Thomas Hardy's Christmas

Andrew Norman

NEW HAVEN PUBLISHING

Published 2023
First Edition
NEW HAVEN PUBLISHING LTD
www.newhavenpublishingltd.com
newhavenpublishing@gmail.com

Cover Design © George Kalchev

new haven

By the Same Author

By Swords Divided: Corfe Castle in the Civil War. Halsgrove, 2003.
Thomas Hardy: Christmas Carollings. Halsgrove, 2005.
Enid Blyton and her Enchantment with Dorset. Halsgrove, 2005.
Tyneham: A Tribute. Halsgrove, 2007.
Agatha Christie: The Finished Portrait. Tempus, 2007.
The Story of George Loveless and
the Tolpuddle Martyrs. Halsgrove, 2008.
Father of the Blind: A Portrait of Sir Arthur Pearson. The History Press, 2009.
Agatha Christie: The Pitkin Guide. Pitkin Publishing, 2009.
Arthur Conan Doyle: The Man behind Sherlock Holmes. The History Press, 2009.
HMS Hood: Pride of the Royal Navy. The History Press, 2009.
Purbeck Personalities. Halsgrove, 2009.
Bournemouth's Founders and Famous Visitors. The History Press, 2010.
Thomas Hardy: Behind the Mask. The History Press, 2011.
A Brummie Boy goes to War. Halsgrove, 2011.
Winston Churchill: Portrait of an Unquiet Mind. Pen & Sword Books, 2012.
Charles Darwin: Destroyer of Myths. Pen & Sword Books, 2013.
Beatrix Potter: Her Inner World. Pen & Sword Books, 2013.
T.E. Lawrence: Tormented Hero. Fonthill, 2014.
Agatha Christie: The Disappearing Novelist. Fonthill, 2014.
Lawrence of Arabia's Clouds Hill. Halsgrove, 2014.
Jane Austen: Love is Like a Rose. Fonthill, 2015.
Kindly Light: The Story of Blind Veterans UK. Fonthill, 2015.
Thomas Hardy at Max Gate: The Latter Years. Halsgrove, 2016.
Corfe Remembered. Halsgrove, 2017.
Thomas Hardy: Bockhampton and Beyond. Halsgrove, 2017.
Mugabe: Monarch of Blood and Tears. Austin Macauley, 2017
Making Sense of Marilyn. Fonthill, 2018.

Hitler's Insanity: A Conspiracy of Silence. Fonthill, 2018.
The Unwitting Fundamentalist. Austin Macauley, 2018.
Robert Mugabe's Lost Jewel of Africa. Fonthill, 2018.
Hitler: Dictator or Puppet? Pen & Sword, 2011, 2020.
Halsewell: A Shipwreck that Gripped the Nation. Fonthill, 2020.
The Amazing Story of Lise Meitner. Pen & Sword, 2021.
Paul Robeson: A Song For Freedom. New Haven Publishing, 2022
Francoise Hardy: A Musical Tale of Love and Loss. New Haven Publishing, 2022.
The Real Sir Arthur Conan Doyle. Pen & Sword, 2023.
A Dorset Childhood: Growing up in the Land of the Tolpuddle Martyrs at the Time of the Cold War. Pen & Sword, 2023.
A Purbeck Romance: Set in Thomas Hardy's Glorious Wessex. Pen & Sword, 2023.

CONTENTS

Here we broached the Christmas barrel,
Pushed up the charred log-ends;
Here we sang the Christmas carol,
And called in friends.

From the poem: *The House of Hospitalities*,
by Thomas Hardy

PREFACE

In the days when labouring classes worked long hours, and for the majority, material comforts were small, Christmas was a time (aside from the formalities of necessary religious observance,) for the exchanging of news, folklore, legend and jokes. For those fortunate enough to be invited to the Hardys' cottage on Christmas Eve, there was the added bonus of food and drink to feed the body, and music – home-made of course – to lift the spirits and nourish the soul.

Hardy's descriptions of such Christmases, as were celebrated by himself and his family, together with his colourful portrayals of characters – in particular the members of the 'Mellstock Quire' (Choir,) whom he described as his favourites - have delighted generations of his readers, and continue to do so.

This then, is the story of Thomas Hardy and of Christmas; of what that greatest of all Christian festivals meant to him, and of how his beliefs changed as the years progressed.

N.B. In order to avoid confusion with his father (Thomas II) and grandfather (Thomas I), Hardy in the early part of this book is referred to as 'Thomas III'.

CHRISTMAS EVE, 1840

It is Christmas Eve, 1840, and a small but dedicated group of people are making their way to a remote thatched cottage at Higher Bockhampton in rural Dorset, to meet and make merry, prior to setting out to sing carols in front of each and every dwelling in the vicinity, as was their time-honoured custom.

Neither the members of the choir who left their footprints in the snow that night, nor those whom they would shortly entertain, could have known that the cottage in which they were shortly to congregate would one day be immortalized as the birthplace of the author and poet Thomas Hardy. In fact Thomas, the first born child of Thomas and Jemima Hardy, had been born only 7 months previously on 2 June 1840, and was currently upstairs, asleep in his cot.

***

The scene, as the singers make their way to what would become universally known as 'Hardy's Cottage' (although Hardy himself preferred to call the dwelling a 'house',) was re-enacted years later by Thomas Hardy in his novel *Under the Greenwood Tree* (published in 1872,) where the parish of Stinsford, in which the cottage was situated, becomes that of 'Mellstock'; the Stinsford Choir becomes the 'Mellstock Quire'; Hardy's Cottage becomes 'Lewgate' - which is occupied not by the Hardy's, but by the Dewy family.

As Dick Dewy, son of Reuben and grandson of William Dewy, is returning to his home 'Lewgate' having, 'just been for a run round by Ewelease Stile and Hollow Hill to warm my feet,'[1] he meets up with fellow 'quire' member Michael Mail.

Presently there emerged from the shade severally five men of different ages and gaits, all of them working villagers of the parish of Mellstock. They represented the chief portion of the Mellstock Parish Choir.[2]

Soon appeared glimmering indications of the few cottages forming the small hamlet of Upper Mellstock for which they were bound, whilst the faint sound of church-bells ringing the Christmas peal could be heard floating over upon the breeze from the direction of Longpuddle [Piddlehinton] and Weatherbury [Puddletown] parishes on the other side of the hills. A little wicket admitted them to the garden, and they proceeded up the path to Dick's house.[3]

The singers consisted of four men and seven boys, upon whom devolved the task of carrying and attending to the lanterns, and holding the books open for the players. Shortly after 10 o'clock the singing-boys arrived at the tranter's house [the men-folk having preceded them], which was invariably the place of meeting, and preparations were made for the start. The older men and musicians wore thick coats, with stiff, perpendicular collars, and coloured handkerchiefs wound round and round the neck till the end came to hand, over all which they just showed their ears and noses like people looking over a wall. The remainder, stalwart ruddy men and boys, were dressed mainly in snow-white smock-frocks, embroidered upon the shoulders and breasts in ornamental forms of hearts, diamonds and zig zags.

***

It should be remembered, that when in later years Hardy reconstructed this scene - which took place when he was but a mere infant - he would have been dependent on the memories of his family, and of his father Thomas II in particular: the latter being a key member of the real-life Stinsford Choir.

HARDY'S COTTAGE

Hardy's birthplace - where he had entered the world in the small bedroom situated at the top of the stairs on 2 June 1840 - and where the fictitious 'Mellstock Quire' traditionally congregated on Christmas Eve, prior to their carollings, was described by Hardy years later in *Under the Greenwood Tree*.

Long [and] low, with a hipped roof of thatch, having dormer windows breaking up into the eaves, a chimney standing in the middle of the ridge and another at each end. [This accords exactly with the real-life Hardy's Cottage in its final form.]

***

Hardy's grandfather Thomas Hardy I, had come to Bockhampton in the year 1801, together with his wife Mary née Head; his father John Hardy of nearby Puddletown (born 1755), having acquired a piece of land and built a house for him there – the present-day cottage. (The Hardy family did not actually own the house; for when they purchased the land and built the dwelling, this was only for the period of their lifetime, or if the landlord permitted, for up to as many as three generations. Such a tenant was therefore called a 'livier'.) Here, Thomas I carried on, 'an old-established building and master-masoning business [i.e. in which he was the manager, contractor, and employer of labour].'[1]   In this occupation he was succeeded in turn by his son Thomas II, who prospered, coming to own, 'a farm, a dozen houses or so, a brickfield [place where bricks are made,] kilns, &c,- all which he preferred to let, having such a liking for the dilapidated old homestead built by his grandfather [i.e. the Hardy cottage at Higher Bockhampton]....' Hardy also noted that, 'the stabling and other outbuildings have been pulled down since his [i.e Thomas II's] time.'[2]

13

In 1839, Thomas II married Jemima Hand of Melbury Osmund. He brought her back to live with him and his widowed mother Mary in the Higher Bockhampton cottage; Thomas I having died in 1837. By 1840, the cottage had been considerably enlarged, and now comprised on the ground floor: an entrance porch, kitchen, parlour, and office; on the first floor were three main bedrooms and one smaller one. In 1841, Hardy's sister Mary was born. She was followed a decade later in 1851 by Henry, then Katharine in 1856.

It was in this cottage that Hardy (Thomas III) at the age of 16, composed his first poem *Domicilium*. Here also, he wrote his first novel *The Poor Man and the Lady*, (which was never published, though parts of it were later used in *Under the Greenwood Tree*.) Also *An Indiscretion in the Life of an Heiress*, *Under the Greenwood Tree* and *Far From the Madding Crowd*, together with portions of *Desperate Remedies and A Pair of Blue Eyes*.

***

Is it possible to gain an insight into life inside Hardy's Cottage in 1841, on the occasion of his first Christmas Eve? Again, yes, because in his novel *Under the Greenwood Tree,* Hardy gives a description of the scene, where members of the 'Mellstock Quire' gather in an atmosphere of warmth and good fellowship, prior to setting off on their rounds of carolling in the parish. On this particular evening,

The fire- and candle-light within radiated forth upon the thick bushes of box and laurestinus growing in clumps outside, and upon the bare boughs of several codlin-trees [varieties of cooking apple] hanging about in various distorted shapes, the result of early training as espaliers combined with careless climbing in to their boughs [presumably by children] in later years.

The choir stamped severally on the door-stone to shake from their boots any fragment of earth or leaf adhering thereto, then entered the house and looked around to survey the condition of things. Through the open doorway of a small inner room on the right hand, of a character between pantry and cellar, was Dick Dewy's father Reuben, by vocation a 'tranter' or irregular carrier, [who is described as] a stout, florid man about forty years of age.

Being now occupied in bending over a hogshead [large cask] that stood in the pantry ready horsed [mounted on a frame] for the process of broaching, he did not take the trouble to turn or raise his eyes at the entry of his visitors, well knowing by their footsteps that they were the expected old comrades.

The main room on the left was decked with bunches of holly and other evergreens, and from the middle of the beam bisecting the ceiling hung the mistletoe, of a size out of all proportion to the room, and extending so low that it became necessary for a full-grown person to walk round it in passing, or run the risk of entangling his hair...

Mrs Dewy sat in a brown settle by the side of the glowing wood fire – so glowing that with a heedful compression of the lips she would now and then rise and put her hand upon the hands and flitches of bacon lining the chimney, to reassure herself that they were not being broiled instead of smoked – a misfortune that had been known to happen now and then at Christmas-time.

'Hullo, my sonnies. Here you be, then!' said Reuben Dewy at length, standing up and blowing forth a vehement gust of breath. 'How the blood do puff up in anybody's head, to be sure, a-stooping like that! I was just going out to [the] gate to hark for ye.' He then carefully began to wind a strip of brown paper round a brass tap he held in his hand. 'This in the cask here is a drop o' the right sort' (tapping the cask); ''tis a real drop o' cordial from the best picked apples – Sansoms, Stubbards, Five-corners and such-like – you d'mind the sort Michael?' (Michael nodded.) 'And there's a sprinkling of they that grow down by the orchard-rails – streaked ones – rail apples wed'call 'em, as 'tis by the rails they grow, and [we] not knowing the right name. The water cider from 'em is as good as most people's best cider is.'

15

'Come in, come in, and draw up to the fire; never mind your shoes,' said Mrs Dewy, seeing that all except Dick had paused to wipe them upon the doormat. 'I am glad that you've stepped up-along at last; and, Susan, you run down to Grammer Kaytes's and see if you can borrow some larger candles than these fourteens [sold at 14 to the pound weight.] Tommy Leaf, don't ye be affeared! Come and sit here in the settle [bench with high back and arms].'[3]

SUPPER AND CAROLLINGS

The holding of a Christmas Eve supper at the Hardy's cottage in Higher Bockhampton was initiated by Hardy's grandfather Thomas I (born 1778,) in order to refresh the members of the local choir - of whom he was one - before they set out to sing carols to their neighbours. This tradition was later carried on by Thomas I's son Thomas II (born 1811,) and one day HIS son Thomas III (Hardy) would also participate in these Christmas festivities.

It was the practice of Thomas II and his choir, to go the northern part of the parish and play at every house before supper; then to return to Bockhampton and sit over the meal till twelve o'clock [midnight], during which interval a good deal was consumed at the Hardy's expense.... Then they started for the other parts of the parish, and did not get home till all was finished at about six in the morning....[1]

Again, the atmosphere is lovingly recreated in every detail in *Under the Greenwood Tree*:

The cider mug was emptied for the ninth time, the music-books were arranged, and the pieces finally decided upon. The boys in the meantime put the old horn-lanterns in order, cut candles into short lengths to fit the lanterns; and, a thin fleece of snow having fallen since the early part of the evening, those who had no leggings went to the stable and wound wisps of hay around their ankles to keep the insidious flakes from the interior of their boots.

Mellstock was a parish of considerable acreage, the hamlets composing it lying at a much greater distance from each other than is ordinarily the case. Hence several hours were consumed in

17

playing and singing within hearing of every family, even if but a single air were bestowed on each. There was Lower Mellstock, the main village; half a mile from this were the church and vicarage, and a few other houses.... A mile north-east lay the hamlet of Upper Melstock, where the tranter lived; and at other points knots of cottages, besides solitary farmsteads and dairies.

Their first port of call is 'Farmer Ledlow's', the journey to which is described in Hardy's inimitable manner:

Just before the clock struck twelve they lighted the lanterns and started. The moon, in her third quarter, had risen since the snowstorm; but the dense accumulation of snow-cloud weakened her power to a faint twilight which was rather pervasive of the landscape than traceable to the sky. The breeze had gone down, and the rustle of their feet and tones of their speech echoed with an alert rebound from every post, boundary-stone, and ancient wall they passed, even where the distance of the echo's origin was less than a few yards. Beyond their own slight noises nothing was to be heard save the occasional bark of foxes in the direction of Yalbury Wood, or the brush of a rabbit among the grass now and then, as it scampered out of their way.

Most of the outlying homesteads and hamlets had been visited by about two o'clock; they then passed across the outskirts of a wooded park towards the main village, nobody being at home at the Manor. Pursuing no recognized track, great care was necessary in walking lest their faces should come in contact with the low-hanging boughs of the old lime-trees, which in many spots formed dense overgrowth of interlaced branches.

There now a follows a discussion amongst the quire members as to the relative merits of various musical instruments. 'Clar'nets... be bad at all times,' said Michael Mail, who described, how one Christmas, on a hard, frosty night, 'the keys of all the clar'nets froze... so that 'twas like drawing a cork every time a key was opened... [and] an icicle o'spet [spit] hung down from the end of every man's clar'net a span long....' Robert Penny agreed:

18

'Clar'nets were not made for the service of the Lard [Lord]; you can see it by looking at 'em….' William Dewy is also of the same mind:

'They should ha' stuck to strings. Your brass-man is a rafting dog – well and good; you're reed-man is a dab at stirring ye - well and good; your drum-man is a rare bowel-shaker – good again. But I don't care who hears me say it, nothing will spak [speak] to your heart wi' the sweetness o' the man of strings!'

Finally, they arrive at the village school where William Dewy calls for a rendering of 'Number seventy-eight' – 'Remember Adam's fall, O thou Man…' - and then, getting no response, for 'Number sixty-four' – 'Rejoice, ye Tenants of the Earth'. Their playing is in vain however, because nobody is at home in the schoolhouse. Despite this setback however, William Dewy said, 'in a clear loud voice, as he had said in the village at that hour and season for the previous forty years – "A merry Christmas to ye!"[2]

***

The sense of pride which the Quire take in observing their musical traditions comes through strongly in the story, as does Hardy's sense of humour (a quality which those who possess only a superficial knowledge of his works

19

AN INCIDENT INVOLVING THE QUIRE

In *Old Andrey's* [Andrew's] *Experience as a Musician*, Hardy describes an unfortunate incident which occurred when the Quire went to entertain the occupants of the manor house. The story is related by one of the musicians:

I was one of the quire-boys at that time, and we and the players were to appear at the manor house as usual that Christmas week, to play and sing in the hall to the squire's people and visitors (among 'em being the archdeacon, Lord and Lady Baxby, and I don't know who); afterwards going, as we always did, to have a good supper in the servants' hall. Andrew [Andrey] knew this was the custom, and meeting us when we were starting to go, he said to us: 'Lord, how I should like to join in that meal of beef, and turkey, and plum-pudding, and ale, that you happy ones be going to just now! One or more less will make no difference to the squire. I am too old to pass as a singing boy, and too bearded to pass as a singing girl; can ye lend me a fiddle, neighbours, that I may come with ye as a bandsman?'

Andrew was duly lent a fiddle, despite the fact that he, 'knew no more of music than the Giant o' Cernel [Cerne Giant - figure carved in chalk in the hill above the village of Cerne Abbas].' Having reached the squire's house, Andrew

made himself as natural as he could in opening the music-books and moving the candles to the best points for throwing light upon the notes; and all went well till we had played and sung 'While Shepherds Watch', and 'Star, Arise', and 'Hark the Glad Sound.'

20

Unfortunately for Andrew however, the squire's mother noticed that he was not playing his instrument along with the others, and asked,
'How is that?' 'I've had a misfortune mem [ma'am],' he says, bowing as meek as a child. 'Coming along the road I fell down and broke my bow.'

On receipt of this news, the squire's mother produced a replacement for Andrew, whereupon he then carried on the pretence of, sawing away with his bow without letting it touch the strings, so that it looked as if he were driving into the tune with heart and soul.

Misfortune struck a second time however, when the archdeacon noticed that Andrew, 'held the fiddle upside down, the nut under his chin, and the tail-piece in his hand....' This caused the audience to, 'crowd round him, thinking 'twas some new way of performing.'

In consequence, Andrew was, 'turned out of the house as a vile imposter,' the squire declaring that he, 'should have notice to leave his cottage that day fortnight.' The squire's wife however relented, and Andrew was admitted again at the back door, having been turned out at the front![1] sometimes accuse him of lacking!) Also, the sheer joy of carolling, is reflected in this lilting poem by Hardy entitled, *The Rash Bride; An Experience of The Mellstock Quire*:

We Christmas-carolled down the Vale, and up the
Vale, and round the Vale
We played and sang that night as we were yearly
wont to do –
A carol in a minor key, a carol in the Major D,
Then at each house: 'Good wishes: many Christmas
joys to you!'

'THE QUIRE': FACT AND FICTION

Hardy mentions by name the members of 'The Mellstock Quire' in his poem: *Winter Night in Woodland*:

And then, when the night has turned twelve the air brings
From dim distance, a rhythm of voices and strings:
'Tis the quire, just afoot on their long yearly rounds,
To rouse by worn carols each house in their bounds;
Robert Penny, the Dewys, Mail, Voss, and the rest; 'til anon
Tired and thirsty, but cheerful, they home to their beds in the
dawn.

The 'Hardy' family.

In describing the activities of 'The Mellstock Quire' in *Under the Greenwood Tree*, Hardy was mirroring the traditions of his own family, who were heavily involved in providing the music for the real life parish of Stinsford, and in particular, in organizing the Christmas Eve entertainment and carolling. For example, whereas in the novel, it is three generations of the 'Dewy' family who are among the chief instrumentalists, so in the real-life Stinsford Choir it was three generations of 'Hardys' who performed this function.

At Stinsford, the Choir's four musicians included Thomas Hardy I (bass cello); his two sons James (born 1805, violin treble) and Thomas II (born 1811, violin tenor); James Dart (born 1812, violin counter, who was James' brother-in-law.) (In fact, Thomas I had previously fulfilled a similar role at his home town of Puddletown, where he had, 'played the violoncello in the church of that parish.')

22

5bStinsford Church. Plan of West Gallery, circa 1835, showing position of Choir. By Thomas Hardy.

Thomas I (died three years before his grandson Thomas III was born,) is said to have given, 'his devoted musical services to Stinsford Church, in which he had occupied the middle seat of the gallery with his base-viol on Sundays for a period of thirty-five years – to no worldly profit; far the reverse, indeed.'[1]

As for the singers (who included boys,) they were [6]described as being 'mainly poor men and hungry', (FEH p.12) and without the generosity of the Hardys they would presumably have passed Christmastime without a proper meal. (Their cause would one day be taken up by Thomas III – as yet a mere infant - in an article published in Longman's Magazine in 1883, entitled *The Dorsetshire Labourer*.)

***

Similarities between members of the Quire and the real life people of Bockhampton.

'Reuben Dewy' (son of 'William') was by vocation a 'tranter' (or irregular carrier.) In real life, William Keats (1799-1870) a tranter, lived with his family directly opposite the Hardys in Cherry Alley (a lane so-called for the obvious reason that it was lined by cherry tress.) It was William who, 'did the haulage of building material for Hardy's father, of [i.e. from] whom he also rented a field for his horses.'[2] Furthermore, in his third notebook, Hardy records the fact that both William Keats and his brother James (born 1808) were members of the Bockhampton band or 'quire'.[3]

'Robert Penny' is described as a boot and shoemaker. (In the story it was he who lent candles to Tranter Reuben's daughter Susan.) According to Hardy, the real life shoemaker and shoe repairer upon whom this character was based was Robert Reason (1763-1819,) whose workshop was situated in Lower Bockhampton.[4]

As for the character 'Voss', who supervises the providing of Christmas Eve refreshments for The Mellstock Quire, Hardy has, for once, used the name of a living person, one 'T. [Thomas] Voss', who lived at Lower Bockhampton. Harold Lionel Voss (who became Hardy's chauffeur) recalls that Thomas Voss (born 1819), who was his grandfather, was, like Thomas Hardy II, also a builder and ornamental plasterer. Hardy's father and my grandfather, sometimes combined forces to tackle a building job that either had to be completed quickly, or [which] would have been too big for either builder separately.

However, Harold Voss states that the real life Voss also had another occupation, one which may only be described as macabre:

I remember hearing how in, I believe, 1887 my grandfather made plaster casts of the heads of the last two men Stone and Preedy, to be publicly hanged at Dorchester.[5]

Whether quire members 'Joseph Bowman' and 'Michael Mail' had real life counterparts is not known.

Other people and places

'Grammer [grandma] Kaytes'. Her name bears a distinct similarity to real-life Rachel Keats (born 1779, the mother of tranter William Keats,) who lived in the next house down the lane from the Hardy's, beyond the paddock. Rachel's son Charles (born 1813) was also a tranter.[6]

'Farmer Ledlow'. The quire on their carollings made his dwelling their first port of call, and it would appear that he corresponds to the real life Joseph Bedloe of Higher Kingston Farm, situated at Higher Bockhampton.

STINSFORD CHURCH AND CHOIR

The cottage at Higher Bockhampton, birthplace of Thomas III (Hardy), was also a focal point for the choir, particularly on Christmas Eve when, 'in addition to the ordinary practice, the work of preparing and copying carols [for] a month of evenings beforehand was not light....'[1] The main purpose of this preparation was of course to enable the choir to perform its official duties of performing at the formal divine services held at Stinsford's church of St Michael, including of course, those held at Christmastime.

When Thomas Hardy I - a musician with the choir of his home town of Puddletown - first arrived in Bockhampton in the year 1801, he discovered to his dismay, that music-making at Stinsford's church was, 'in a deplorable condition.' Accordingly he, immediately set himself, with the easy-going vicar's hearty concurrence, to improve it, and got together some instrumentalists, himself taking the bass–viol [cello] as before, which he played in the gallery of Stinsford's parish church at two services every Sunday from 1801 or 1802 till his death in 1837, being joined later by his two sons....[2]

In this case, the vicar in question was the Rev. Edward Murray, described as, an ardent musician and performer on the violin himself, and the two younger Hardys and sometimes their father, used to practise two or three times a week with him in his study at Stinsford House, where he lived instead of at the Vicarage.

Such was the excellence of the, 'Hardy instrumentalists' that they, 'maintained an easy superiority over the larger bodies in parishes near[by].' Thomas I however, being an unselfish man, would go whenever opportunity served and assist other choirs by performing with his violoncello in the galleries of their parish churches, mostly to the high contentment of the congregation.[3]

***

Having left his first school at Bockhampton, Thomas III transferred to Dorchester's Nonconformist British School for Boys. Nevertheless on Sundays, he was kept strictly at church… as usual, till he knew the Morning and Evening Services by heart, including the rubrics [directions for the conduct of divine service,] as well as large portions of the New Version of the Psalms.[4]

Is it possible to recapture a flavour of what a Christmas service at Stinsford Church (where incidentally the Hardy family had its own pews) was like in those days? The answer is yes, because Hardy described it vividly in *A Few Crusted Characters*, (published 1894,) where Stinsford becomes the customary 'Mellstock'. This story also gives Hardy another opportunity to demonstrate his sense of humour! The 'Mellstock Parish Players', described as, 'all sound and powerful musicians, and strong-winded men,' were very much in demand [in] Christmas week for little reels and dancing parties: for they could turn a jig or a hornpipe out of hand as well as ever they could turn out a psalm…. In short, one half-hour they could be playing a Christmas carol in the Squire's hall to the ladies and gentlemen, and drinking tay [tea] and coffee with 'em as modest as saints; and the next at The Tinker's Arms, blazing away like wild horses with the 'Dashing white Sergeant' to nine couple of dancers and more, and swallowing rum-and–cider hot as flame.

However, this particular Christmas the quire had been, 'out to one rattling randy after another every night, and had got next to no sleep at all.' Another problem for them was that the Sunday after Christmas, when they were due to play for the service, the weather was, so mortal cold… that they could hardly sit in the gallery; for though the congregation down in the body of the church had a stove to keep off the frost, the players in the gallery had nothing at all. So Nicholas [Puddingcome]   said at morning service, when 'twas freezing an inch an hour, 'Please the Lord I won't stand this numbing weather no longer: this afternoon we'll have something in our insides to make us warm, if it cost a king's ransom.

So he brought a gallon of hot brandy and beer, ready mixed, to church with him in the afternoon, and by keeping the jar well wrapped up in Timothy Thomas' bass-viol bag it kept drinkably warm till they wanted it, which was just a thimbleful in the Absolution, and another after the Creed, and the remainder at the beginning o' the sermon. When they'd had the last pull they felt quite comfortable and warm, and as the sermon went on – most unfortunately for 'em it was a long one that afternoon – they fell asleep, every man jack of 'em; and there they slept on as sound as rocks.

'Twas a very dark afternoon, and by the end of the sermon all you could see of the inside of the church were the pa'son's two candles alongside of him in the pulpit, and his spaking [speaking] face behind 'em. The sermon being ended at last, the pa'son gie'd [gived] out the Evening Hymn. But no quire set about sounding up the tune, and the people began to turn their heads to learn the reason why, and then Levy Limpet, a boy who sat in the gallery, nudged Timothy [Thomas] and Nicholas and said, 'Begin! Begin!'.

'Hey? What?' said Nicholas, starting up; and the church being so dark and his head so muddled he thought he was at the party they had played at all the night before, and away he went, bow and fiddle, at *The Devil among the Tailors*, the favourite jig of our neighbourhood at that time. The rest of the band, being in the same state of mind and nothing doubting, followed their leader with all their strength, according to custom. They poured out that there tune till the lower bass notes of *The Devil*

THE DEMISE OF THE CHOIR

Edward Murray (a relation of the Earl of Ilchester, patron of Stinsford) was Vicar of Stinsford from 1823 to 1837. Murray's connection with the Hardy family was a close one, for not only did he encourage them in their music, but from 1836, he also employed Thomas II's wife Jemima as his cook.

This happy relationship however, was not to last: the demise of Stinsford's choir coinciding with the appointment of a youthful new vicar Arthur G Shirley, aged 26, who succeeded Murray in 1937. Having, as an undergraduate at Oxford, been influenced by the 'High Church' leaders (namely John Keble, John Newman and Edward Pusey,) Shirley now proceeded to put their ideas into practice at Stinsford. (Thomas Hardy I did not live to witness the tragic event which was now to befall his beloved choir, for he died in that very same year.)

In, 'a sweeping restoration' performed in the early 1840s, not only did Shirley remove the church's chancel pews, but he replaced the choir and its string musicians with a barrel organ; an action viewed by the Hardy family as nothing less than vandalism, for which they never forgave him. Hardy himself described this as a 'disastrous restoration…,' when the 'excellent old oak pews of Caroline or early Georgian date were swept away….' The final insult came in 1843, when the major part of the west gallery was removed.

(By contrast with Stinsford, the church of St Mary's in Puddletown, Hardy's grandfather Thomas I's home town, escaped restoration and retained its musicians' gallery dating from 1635; its original pulpit and pews; its inscribed brass memorial plates; its Norman font, and its effigies of knights and their ladies.)

The effect on the Choir of these unhappy events is also reflected in *Under the Greenwood Tree*, where the vicar 'Mr Maybold' represents the infamous Reverend Shirley:

'Times have changed from the times they used to be,' said [Michael] Mail. 'People don't care much about us now! I've been thinking we must be almost the last left in the county of the old string players? Barrel-organs, and the things next door to 'em that you blow wi' your foot, have come in terribly of late years.'

'Aye!' said [Joseph] Bowman, shaking his head; and old William, on seeing him, did the same thing.

'More's the pity,' replied another. 'Time was – long and merry ago now – when not one of the varmits [varmints] was to be heard of; but it served some of the quires right. They should have stuck to strings as we did, and keep [kept] out clarinets, and done away with serpents. If you'd thrive in musical religion, stick to strings, says I.'[1]

The destruction of the Stinsford Choir is again alluded to by Hardy in *Life's Little Ironies*. Here, the fictitious name 'Longpuddle' replaces Stinsford, and the action of the vicar is construed as a punishment for the 'quire' on account of them having fallen asleep during his sermon. 'It happened on Sunday after Christmas – the last Sunday ever they played in Longpuddle church gallery, as it turned out, though they didn't know it then.' The barrel-organ is described as one, that would play two-and-twenty new psalm-tunes, so exact and particular that, however sinful inclined you was, you could play nothing but psalm-tunes whatsomever. He [the vicar] had a really respectable man to turn the winch… and the old players played no more.'[2]

***

It has to be said that even when the Choir ceased to exist, the Hardy family did not entirely turn its back on music-making at Stinsford Church, for as Hardy's sister Katharine observed,

29

After the old choir came to an end, Uncle James Hardy worked the barrel-organ in Stinsford Choir for 40 years. [James died in 1880.] From 1880 onward, his daughter Theresa played [the] harmonium for 40 years.'[3] *among the Tailors* made the cobwebs in the roof shiver like ghosts; then Nicholas, seeing nobody moved, shouted out as he scraped, 'Top couples cross hands! And when I make the fiddle squeak at the end, every man kiss his pardner [partner] under the mistletoe!'

'The unfortunate church band came to their senses, and remembered where they were; and 'twas a sight to see Nicholas Puddingcome and Timothy Thomas and John Biles creep down the gallery stairs with their fiddles under their arms, and poor Dan'l Hornhead with his serpent [a bass wind instrument, so-called because of its shape] and Robert Dowdle with his clarionet, all looking as little as ninepins; and out they went.'[5]

Finally, the school referred to in *Under the Greenwood Tree* clearly represents Hardy's first school at Lower Bockhampton.

***

Following the demise of the beloved members of his 'Mellstock Quire', Hardy imagined them to be lying in 'Mellstock (i.e. Stinsford) Churchyard', the very place where his own ancestors and fellow-villagers had been buried. Witness his poem *The Dead Quire*;

> Old Dewy lay by the gaunt yew tree,
> And Reuben and Michael a pace behind,
> And Bowman with his family
> By the wall that the ivies bind.

THE SHOW GOES ON!

The fact that from 1842, it was no longer possible for Thomas Hardy II and the members of his Stinsford Choir to play in Stinsford Church, meant that Sundays and other days of Christian observance could never be the same again. This was felt particularly poignantly at Christmastime, normally intended to be the most joyous of all Christian festivals in the year.

The Hardy family's interest in music stretched back even prior to the time of Thomas I, in that another ancestor, also named Thomas, who lived in Dorchester in 1724, was a subscriber to 'Thirty Select Anthems in Score' by Dr W Croft, organist of the Chapel Royal and Westminster Abbey.)[1] In the light of events at Stinsford, one might imagine that for the young Hardy (then only in his second year of life,) there would be little prospect of following in his father's and grandfather's footsteps. The Hardy family however, was not to be silenced so easily!

Thomas II was determined to encourage his son to be musical, and to this end presented him, when he was 4 years old, with the gift of a small accordion inscribed with his name 'Thomas Hardy' and the date '1844'. 'Under his father's instruction [Hardy] was soon able to tweedle [make the sound] from notation, some hundreds of jigs and country-dances that he found in his father's and grandfather's old books.' That he had a good ear for music is confirmed by the fact, that as a boy he tuned fiddles (a fiddle being an instrument similar to a violin but with a raised fingerboard and higher bridge) and, 'went on as a youth in his teens, to keep his mother's old table-piano in tune whenever he had the time....'[2] In fact the young Hardy is described as being, 'extraordinarily sensitive to music,' so much so that, among the endless jigs, hornpipes, reels, waltzes, and country-dances that his father played of an evening in his [Thomas II's] early married years, and to which the boy danced a *pas seul* in the middle of the room, there were three or four that always moved the child to tears, though he strenuously tried to hide them.[3]

Therefore, by the time Hardy was aged 20, he was a proficient enough performer to rush off in the evening, with his fiddle under his arm, sometimes in the company of his father as first violin and his uncle [James – then aged 54, described as 'bricklayer of Higher Bockhampton' who was married to Jane and had three sons (1841 census)] as cellist, to play... at an agriculturist's wedding, christening, or Christmas party in a remote dwelling among the fallow fields, not returning sometimes till nearly dawn, the Hardys still being traditionally string-bandsmen available on such occasions, and having the added recommendation of charging nothing for their services, which was a firm principal with them....[4]

Therefore, the Hardy family, although denied the opportunity to display their musicianship in the formal setting of Stinsford Church, continued to entertain at parties and dances held at various locations throughout the Parish.

It is recorded that Hardy's, physical vigour was now much greater than it had been when he was a child, and it enabled him, like a conjuror at a fair, to keep in the air the three balls of architecture, scholarship, and dance-fiddling, without ill effects, the fiddling being of course not daily, like the other two.[5]

***

One such Christmas party, held at tranter Dewy's house, was described by Hardy in *Under the Greenwood Tree*, when as soon as Christmas Day is over, the revelry can begin. Not only that, there is a hint of romance in the air!

The guests had all assembled, and the tranter's party had reached that degree of development which accords with ten o'clock p.m. in rural assemblies. At that hour the sound of a fiddle in process of tuning was heard from the inner pantry. 'That's Dick,' said the tranter. 'That lad's crazy for a jig.' However, Dick's father William restrains him:

'I cannot have any dancing at all till Christmas-day is out. When the clock ha' done striking twelve, dance as much as ye like.' These sentiments were supported by Mrs Penny. 'If you do have a party on Christmas-night, 'tis only fair and honourable to the sky-folk [possibly a reference to the 'sky god' of Celtic mythology] to have a sit-still party. Jigging parties be all very well on the Devil's holidays; but a jigging party looks suspicious now. Oh yes; stop till the clock strikes, young folk – so say I.'

Finally, the clock strikes twelve and the instrumentalists, with 'old William very readily taking the bass-viol from its accustomed nail, and touching the strings as irreligiously as could be desired,' start the proceedings with a country-dance called 'Triumph, or Follow my Lover.' The tempo increases the, 'fiddlers as well as the dancers get red in the face,' and as the latter advance 'further still towards incandescence... the fiddlers no longer sit down, but kick back their chairs and saw madly at the strings with legs firmly spread and eyes closed, regardless of the visible world.'[6]

For Dick Dewy, on this Boxing Day morning, there is the added excitement of love in the offing, in the shape of the 'comely, slender, prettily-dressed prize Fancy Day.'[7]

Again and again did Dick... promenade in a circle with her [Fancy] all to himself, his arm holding her waist more firmly each time, and his elbow getting further and further behind her back, till the distance reached was rather noticeable; and, most blissful, swinging to places shoulder to shoulder, her breath curling round his neck like a summer zephyr that had strayed from its proper date. Threading the couples one by one they reached the bottom, when there arose in Dick's mind a minor misery lest the tune should end before they could work their way to the top again, and have anew the same exciting run down through. Dick's feelings on actually reaching the top in spite of his doubts were supplemented by a mortal fear that the fiddling might even stop at this supreme moment; which prompted him to convey a stealthy whisper to the far-gone musicians to the effect that they were not to leave off till he and his partner had reached the bottom of the dance once more.... Fancy was now held so closely that Dick and she were practically one person [and] the room became to Dick like picture in a dream.... [UGT p.83.]

(Surely in this story, Hardy is reflecting not only his own enjoyment of the dance, but also his propensity to fall in love, which was one of his well-known characteristics!)

SCANT REWARD FOR THE QUIRE:
'THE PAPHIAN BALL'

Something of the tremendous effort which the quire put in, compared with the paltriness of the reward it received, is indicated by Hardy in the preface to his novel *Under the Greenwood Tree*.

The zest of these bygone instrumentalists must have been keen and staying, to take them as it did, on foot every Sunday after a toilsome week through all weathers to the church, which often lay at a distance from their homes. They usually received so little in payment for their performances that their efforts were really a labour of love. In the parish I had in my mind when writing the present tale, the gratuities received yearly by the musicians at Christmas were somewhat as follows: from the manor house ten shillings and a supper; from the vicar ten shillings; from the farmers five shillings each; from each cottage-household one shilling; amounting altogether to not more than ten shillings a head annually - just enough, as an old executant [performer of music] told me, to pay for their fiddle-strings, repairs, rosin and music-paper (which they mostly ruled themselves.) Their music in those days was all in their own manuscript, copied in the evenings after work, and their music-books were home-bound.

The aforesaid fiddle-strings, rosin, and music-paper were supplied by a pedlar, who travelled exclusively in such wares from parish to parish, coming to each village about every six months. Tales are told of the consternation once caused among the church fiddlers when, on the occasion of their producing a new Christmas anthem, he did not come to time, owing to being snowed-up on the downs, and the straits they were in through having to make shift with whipcord and twine for strings.[1]

When, in September 1924, (publisher) Sir Frederick Macmillan requested a poem relating to Christmas, to be published in McCall's magazine, Hardy offered him, *The Midnight Revel* (later retitled *The Paphian Ball: Another Christmas Experience of the Mellstock Quire*.) As has already been noted, the real-life Choir was poorly rewarded for its efforts, and the Hardy family in particular made a point of not accepting any payment whatsoever for its services.

In *The Paphian Ball*, as the characters of the Mellstock Quire duly set out on their Christmas rounds, they are tempted by riches (by a figure who presumably represents the Devil,) to succumb to this temptation, are denied their reward, and are finally granted redemption:

> We went our Christmas rounds once more,
> With quire and viols as theretofore.
> Our path was near by Rushy-pond,
> Where Egdon-Heath outstretched beyond.

However, by Rushy Pond they encounter a figure, silhouetted against the moon, who ridicules them for their Christmas carollings:

These ancient hymns in the freezing night, And all for nought? 'Tis foolish, quite!

Instead, the figure offers them an inducement to 'come and [play the] lute at a ball…,' saying:

> Tis to your gain, for it ensures
> That many guineas will be yours.'

The Quire members are duly blindfolded and lured to, 'a strange hall,' with,

> Gilded alcoves, great chandeliers,
> Voluptuous paintings ranged in tiers.

36

In brief, a mansion large and rare,
With rows of dancers waiting there.

Here,

They tuned and played; the couples danced;
Half-naked women tripped, advanced,

And thus and thus the slow hours wore then:
While shone their guineas heaped before them.

Suddenly however, the Quire is brought back to reality:

And in a moment, at a blink,
There flashed a change; ere they could think.

The ball-room vanished and all its crew:
Only the well-known heath they view -

Yea; the rare mansion, gorgeous, bright,
The ladies, gallants, gone were quite.

The heaped-up guineas, too, were gone
With the gold table they were on.

The Quire now have no choice but to return home. However,
when they appear in church the following morning, they are
given a surprise by the congregation:

With downcast heads and scarce a word,
They were astound at what they heard.

Praises from all came forth in showers
For how they'd cheered the midnight hours.

'We've heard you many times,' friends said; 'But like that never
have you played!

Rejoice, ye tenants of the Earth,
And celebrate your Saviour's birth,

Never so thrilled the darkness through,
Or more inspired us so to do!'

THE MUMMERS

Christmas for Thomas Hardy and his family and friends would not have been the same without the presence of the Christmas mummers (a mummer being defined as an actor in a traditional masked mime or folk-play.)

According to Hardy, the mummers - who numbered from twelve to fifteen - all men and boys, including, "the fair Sabra" would go to the farmhouses round, between Christmas and Twelfth Night, doing some four or five performances each evening, and getting ale and money at every house. Sometimes the mummers of one village would encroach on the traditional 'sphere of influence' of another village and then there would be a battle in good earnest.[1]

Hardy gave a detailed description, with illustrations, of how the mummers attired themselves. 'The surcoat or tunic was formed of a white smock frock, rather shorter than usual, tied in round the waist by a strap – this was almost invariably the groundwork of the costume....

The helmet was made of pasteboard, & was much like one of those articles called 'tea-cosys' which people use now a days for keeping the tea-pot warm, with a tuft at the top. The sword was wood, of course, & the *staff*, which was never dispensed with, consisted of a straight stick the size of a broom handle, 5 or 6 feet long, with small sticks inserted cross wise at the upper end: from the end of these small sticks paper tassels dangled.[2]

In *The Return of the Native*, Hardy described the excitement which the arrival of the mummers evoked in the local population:

At this moment the fiddles finished off with a screech, and the serpent emitted a last note that nearly lifted the roof. When, from the comparative quiet within, the mummers judged that the dancers had taken their seats, Father Christmas advanced, lifted the latch, and put his head inside the door.

'Ah, the mummers, the mummers!' cried several guests at once. 'Clear a space for the mummers.'

Hump-backed Father Christmas then made a complete entry, swinging his huge club, and in a general way clearing the stage for the actors proper, while he informed the company in smart verse that he was come, welcome or welcome not; concluding his speech with,

'Make room, make room, my gallant boys,
And give us space to rhyme;
We've come to show St George's play,
Upon this Christmas time.'

The guests were now arranging themselves at one end of the room, the fiddler was mending a string, the serpent-player was emptying his mouthpiece, and the play began.[3]

Hardy stated that,

Our mummers hereabouts gave a regular performance. *The Play of St George*, it was called. It contained quite a number of traditional characters: the valiant soldier, the Turkish knight, St George himself, the Saracen, Father Christmas, the fair Sabra and so on. Rude as it was, the thing used to impress me very much – I can clearly recall the odd sort of thrill it would give. The performers used to carry a long staff in one hand and a wooden sword in the other, and pace monotonously round in toning their parts on one note, and punctuating them by nicking the sword against the staff – something like this: 'Here come I, the valiant soldier (nick), Slasher is my name (nick).'

40

He could not recall the action of the play, except that it ended in a series of mortal combats in which all the characters but St George were killed. And then the curious thing was that they were invariably brought to life again. The personage was introduced for the purpose – [namely] the doctor of physic, wearing a cloak and a broad brimmed beaver [hat].

In *The Return of the Native*, Hardy described how during preparations for a forthcoming performance of the play of 'St George' by the mummers, there was scope for a little behind the scenes romance!

It might be that Joe, who fought on the side of Christendom, had a sweetheart, and that Jim, who fought on the side of the Moslem, had one likewise. During the making of the costumes it would come to the knowledge of Joe's sweetheart that Jim's was putting brilliant silk scallops at the bottom of her lover's surcoat, in addition to the ribbons of the visor, the bars of which, being invariably formed of coloured strips about half an inch wide hanging before the face, were mostly of that material. Joe's sweetheart straightway placed brilliant silk on the scallops of the hem in question, and going a little further, added ribbon tufts to the shoulder pieces. Jim's, not to be outdone, would affix bows and rosettes everywhere.

The result was that in the end, the valiant soldier, of the Christian army, was distinguished by no peculiarity of accoutrement from the Turkish knight; and what was worse, on a casual view St George himself might be mistaken for his deadly enemy, the Saracen.[4]

***

In the preface to his epic, dramatic composition *The Dynasts*, Hardy, who until the end of his days, enjoyed the performances of the Christmas mummers, described their, '…curiously hypnotizing impressiveness,' and an 'automatic style' which was, 'that of persons who spoke by no will of their own….'[5] Perhaps it was the mummers who gave Hardy the idea which is central to *The Dynasts* in which a great force, which he calls, the 'urging immanence' continually manipulates the peoples of the Earth as if they were puppets.[6]

FROM ARCHITECT TO WRITER: MARRIAGE

Hardy's progression from schoolboy to writer came about as follows: in 1856, at the age of 16, he commenced a 3 year course as pupil at the office of John Hicks, architect and church restorer of Dorchester. The following year his grandmother Mary died, leaving all her property including the Bockhampton cottage to her third son (Hardy's father Thomas II,) the elder two having already married and left home.

Having completed the architectural course, Hardy was subsequently employed in 1859, as a church surveyor and restorer, a position about which he had mixed feelings, having heard how the Reverend Shirley had devastated Stinsford Church in the name of 'restoration'. In April 1862, Hardy moved to London, and the following month commenced as an assistant to architect Arthur W Blomfield.

Although Hardy would find himself living at a variety of different locations over the course of the forthcoming years, it appears from his letters that whenever possible, he preferred to spend Christmas at the family home at Higher Bockhampton. For example, to his sister Mary in November 1862 he wrote, 'I suppose you are very glad that Xmas is coming…. I expect to come home [from London] for Xmas, for a little time.'[1]

In July 1867, Hardy returned to Dorset due to ill health, and resumed work at the Dorchester office of John Hicks. However, the work was sporadic, so he used his spare time to write his first novel *The Poor Man and the Lady*. Hicks died in the winter of 1868, and the following summer Hardy commenced work for GR Crickmay, architect of Weymouth. In March 1870 he was sent by

Crickmay to survey the church of St Juliot, near Boscastle in North Cornwall, and it was here that he met his wife-to-be Emma Lavinia Gifford (who was born in the same year as Hardy himself.)

May 1870 found Hardy once more in London, assisting architect Blomfield. That August he revisited Cornwall to check on the restoration work at the church of St Juliot, and to renew his courtship of Emma. *Desperate Remedies* was his first novel to be published, on 25 March 1871. He returned to London again in the spring of 1872; *Under the Greenwood Tree* being published that June. In August, Hardy returned to Dorset to commence work on *A Pair of Blue Eyes*, which was inspired by his visit to Cornwall. This novel was published in May 1873, when Hardy was aged 32.

The Christmas of 1873 found Hardy visiting Emma at St Juliot. In that year he had sustained a great personal loss, with the death by suicide on 21 September of his great friend and mentor Horace Moule. An author and a reviewer of books, who was senior to Hardy by 8 years, Horace was the son of the esteemed vicar of Fordington (Dorchester,) the Reverend Henry Moule. Hardy had visited him only 6 months previously at Cambridge where he was a fellow of Queens' College. After Horace's death, Hardy quoted from Psalm 74: 'Not one is there among us that understandeth any more.'[2]

***

Hardy appears to have had cordial relationships with his wife Emma's sister Helen and her husband the Reverend Caddell Holder, Rector of St Juliot. However, there was great antipathy on the part of Emma's father John Attersoll Gifford, solicitor, who described Hardy as 'that low-born churl who has presumed to marry into my family.'[3] There were problems too on Hardy's side of the family in that his mother Jemima and his father Thomas II seemed unable to strike up any meaningful relationship with Emma, let alone with her parents, and vice-versa.

44

It comes as no surprise therefore, that when Hardy and Emma were married on 17 September 1874 at St Peter's Church, Paddington - where Hardy was living at the time - neither his parents nor hers attended the wedding. In fact, the only people present, apart from the couple, were Emma's uncle Edwin Hamilton Gifford, Canon of Worcester, (who married them,) Emma's brother Walter, and the daughter of Hardy's landlady (who signed the book as a witness.)[4]

EARLY YEARS WITH EMMA

Having visited Brighton and the Continent, Hardy and Emma began their married life in rented accommodation at St David's Villa, Hook Road, Surbiton, Surrey. (It was at about this time that Hardy decided to give up the practice of architecture in favour of writing.) In November 1874, *Far from the Madding Crowd* was published. In March 1875, the couple moved to Westbourne Grove, Paddington.

July 1875 found Hardy and Emma at West End Cottage, Swanage, Dorset, where *The Hand of Ethelberta* was completed. For the next decade, they would reside at a succession of different locations, each of which would provide Hardy with inspiration for his novels.

After a brief sojourn in Yeovil, Somerset, they moved, in July 1876, to lodgings at Riverside Villa, Sturminster Newton, which in turn inspired *The Return of the Native*, - a novel which reflected Hardy's lifelong fascination with the Napoleonic wars. That Christmas they stayed with Hardy's parents at Bockhampton, which was apparently when Emma met his parents for the first time. March 1878 found the couple again back in London, Hardy having concluded that this is where he must live if he were to succeed as a writer.

Tensions between the two families continued, largely on account of Emma and her father's feelings of superiority to the Hardys, and of Emma's particular dislike for Hardy's sister Mary (headmistress of the Bell St Junior School, Dorchester,) whom she described as a 'witch-like' creature.[1] Despite this however, Hardy's father Thomas II remained well disposed towards the couple, declaring

46

on the last day of the year 1878, that he had, 'drunk both their healths in gin and rhubarb wine, with hopes that they would live to see many and many a New Year's Day.'[2]

June 1881, brought another move, this time to Wimborne in Dorset. (From now on, they would visit the capital for a few months only each year.) In that year, *A Laodicean* was published; followed in 1882 by *Two on a Tower*. June 1883 found the couple living in Dorchester.

A PEAL OF BELLS

At Christmastime one of Hardy's chief joys was to listen to the church bells as they rang in the New Year. For example on 31 December 1884, he recorded in his diary,

To St Peter's [Church, Dorchester] belfry to the New-Year's-Eve ring. The night-wind whisked in through the louvers [of the belfry] as the men prepared the mufflers with tar-twine and pieces of horse-cloth. [They] Climbed over the bells to fix the mufflers. I climbed with them and looked into the tenor bell: it is worn into a bright pit where the clapper has struck it so many years, and the clapper is battered with its many blows.

The ringers now put their coats and waistcoats and hats upon the chimes and clock and stand too. Old John is fragile, as if the bell would pull him up rather than he pull the rope down, his neck being withered and white as his white neckcloth. But his manner is severe as he says, 'Tenor out?' One of the two tenor-men gently eases the bell forward – that fine old E flat, my father's admiration, unsurpassed in metal all the world over – and answers, 'Tenors out.' Then old John tells them to, 'Go!' and they start. Through long practice he rings with the least possible movement of his body, though the youngest ringer's – strong, dark-haired men with ruddy faces – soon perspire with their exertion. The red, green, and white sallies [bell ropes] bolt up through the holes like rats between the huge beams overhead.

The grey stones of the fifteenth-century masonry have many of their joints mortarless, and are carved with many initials and dates. On the sill of one louvred window stands a great pewter pot with a hinged cover and engraved: 'For the use of the ringers 16-'.[1]

Although the last two digits on the pewter pot are missing, it is known that the bells themselves predate it, a 'Return of Church Goods' for the year 1550 recording that the tower then contained five 'greate belles'.[2] (When this number was subsequently increased by three, the church became the first in Dorset to boast a ring of eight bells.)

Hardy's Cottage. The National Trust.

Thomas Hardy senior,
oil on canvas by Mary Hardy.
Dorset County Museum.

Jemima Hardy,
oil on canvas by Mary Hardy.
Dorset County Museum.

Thomas Hardy's birthplace, sketch by Thomas Hardy.

'Dick Dewy'. R. Knight.

'Michael Mail'. R. Knight.

'The Tranter'. R. Knight.

'Thomas Leaf'. R. Knight.

'Going the Rounds'. R. Knight.

'Grandfather William'. R. Knight.

'The Quire'. R. Knight.

'Mr Penny'. R. Knight.

'Fancy Day'. R. Knight.

STINSFORD CHURCH.

Plan of West Gallery – circa 1835, Shewing Positions of Choir.

Explanation

T.H. sen.	Tho. Hardy	b. 1778. d. 1837.
T.H. jun.	Tho. Hardy	b. 1811. d. 1892
J.H.	James Hardy	b. 1805. d. 188–.
J.D.	James Dart	b. 181–. d. 187–.

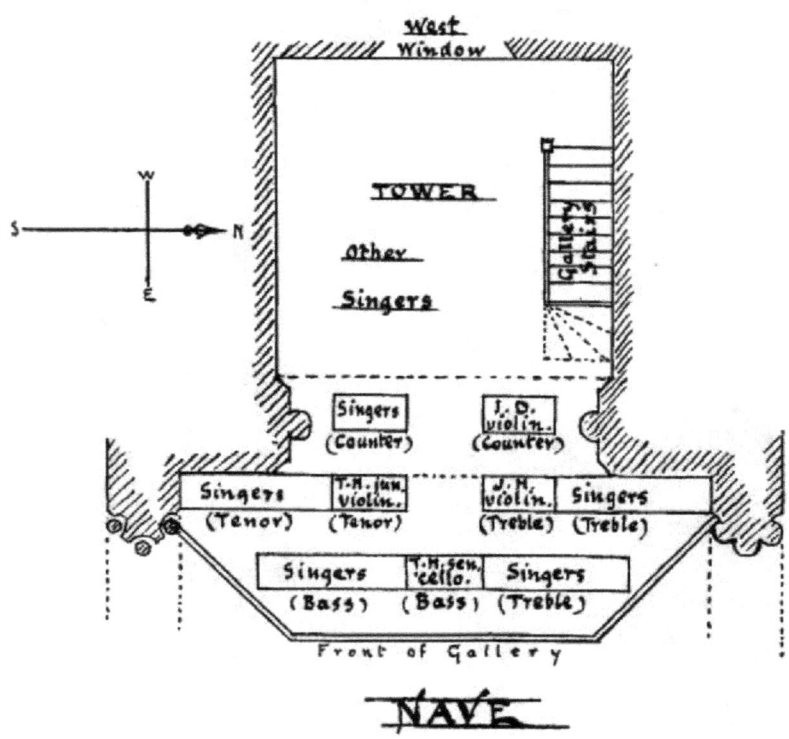

West Window

TOWER

Other Singers

Gallery Stairs

W — N — S — E

Singers (Counter)	J.D. violin. (Counter)

Singers (Tenor)	T.H. jun. violin. (Tenor)	J.H. violin. (Treble)	Singers (Treble)

Singers (Bass)	T.H. sen. 'cello. (Bass)	Singers (Treble)

Front of Gallery

NAVE

Del.   Th.H.

Stinsford Church.
Plan of West Gallery, circa 1835 showing position of the choir, by Thomas Hardy.

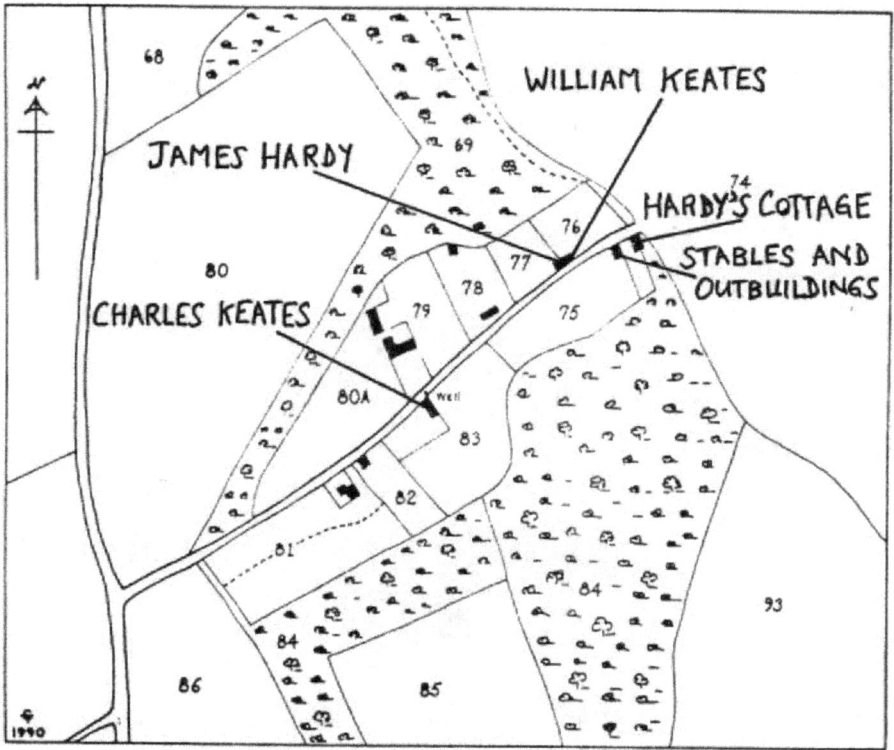

Inhabitants of 'Cherry Alley', Higher Bockhampton,
from the Tithe Commissioners map of 1839.

Stinsford's Church of St Michael.

Stinsford Church prior to its restoration, showing Old West Gallery,
sketch by Thomas Hardy.

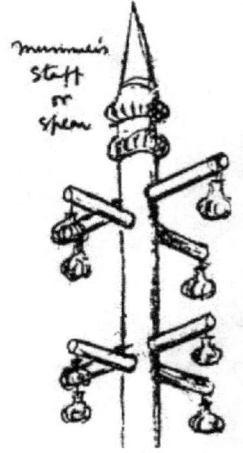

Mummer's costumes, sketch by Thomas Hardy.

Mummer's staff,
sketch by Thomas
Hardy.

Thomas Hardy in 1861.
Dorset County Museum.

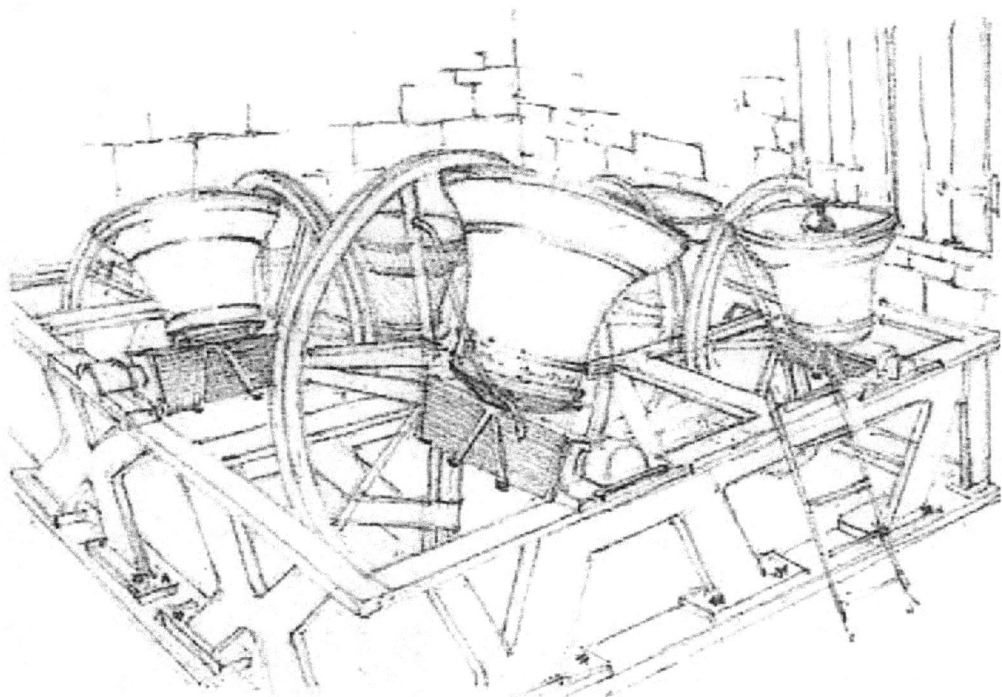

St Peter's church bells. John Herring.

Max Gate. Andrew Leah.

"Mary card"

CRISZES MÆSSE

A·TIME ·TO· WIME

TO·LAVGH·TO·GOOD

MCMII.

WITH·BEST·WISHES   FROM T.H.

Christmas card, designed by Thomas Hardy
(a facsimile of the sun dial attached to the front wall of Max Gate),
to his sisters Mary and Katharine, 24 December 1902. Dorset County Museum.

Bench Ends – St. Juliot Church – Cornwall.
1870.

T. Hardy. del.

Pews at St Juliot Church, Cornwall, which did not survive the 'restoration' of 1870,
sketch by Thomas Hardy. Rector and Churchwardens of St Juliot.

Thomas Hardy.
Mary Evans Picture Library.

GREETINGS - - - from
Mr. and Mrs. THOMAS HARDY

'Greetings from Mr and Mrs Thomas Hardy',
Christmas 1923,
card designed by Thomas Hardy and featuring
Max Gate and the terrier 'Wessex'.

MAX GATE.
DORCHESTER. XMAS. 1926.

WITH THE THOUGHTS
OF T.H. & F.E.H.

Nellie. with best wishes.

'From Mr and Mrs Hardy to Nellie [Titterington] with best wishes', Christmas 1926,
card designed by Thomas Hardy and again featuring Max Gate and 'Wessex'.

Tomb in Stinsford Churchyard where Thomas Hardy's heart is buried.
His body lies in 'Poet's Corner', Westminster Abbey.

MAX GATE

On 29 June 1885, the couple moved to Max Gate, a house designed by Hardy (and built for him by his brother Henry) on the outskirts of Dorchester. Neither Hardy's parents, nor his brother or sisters ever visited him there; the reason being that Emma did not welcome them. New Year's Eve 1885, 'finds me sadder than many previous New Year's Eves have done,' said Hardy, and began to doubt, 'whether building this house at Max Gate was a wise expenditure of energy....'[1]

Hardy's barber WG Mills, stated that in the early years, Hardy visited him at his hairdressing saloon, but later the latter called at his house Max Gate, where the hair-cutting was performed in the drawing room, for the fee of 1 shilling and sixpence. 'Hardy never gave a tip nor a Christmas present... he was very close with his money,' he said.[2]

Hardy described the winter of 1886 (the year in which *The Mayor of Casterbridge* was published) in his own inimitable way.

The landscape has turned from a painting to an engraving: the birds that love worms fall back upon berries: the back parts of homesteads assume, in the general nakedness of the trees, a humiliating squalidness as to their details that has not been contemplated by their occupiers.[3]

'A Merrie Xmas to you, & to ye family,' wrote Hardy to his friend the poet and critic Edmund Gosse, that Christmas Eve. 'I am trying to feel up to the level of the above, but come short of it a little.' He then voiced his displeasure at the way the critics had treated his recently published novel *Far from the Madding Crowd*:

Literature certainly is in rather a bad way, but perhaps a time will come when a scientific system of reviewing will be adopted, & books no longer condemned in their entirety for some reason as that the critic finds a slip in an accent, quotation, or date. My last novel was sneered at by the Saturday [*Saturday Review*] because of a sentence describing a rather unlikely way of improving bad flour, which had scarcely anything to do with the story.[4]

1887 saw the publication of *The Woodlanders*. On Christmas Day 1890, Hardy in more cheerful mood, stated: 'While thinking of resuming, "the viewless wings of poesy" before dawn this morning, new horizons seemed to open and worrying pettiness to disappear.' That New Year's Eve, he records that he,

Looked out of doors just before twelve, and was confronted by the toneless white of the snow spread in front, against which stood the row of pines breathing out: "'Tis no better with us than with the rest of creation, you see!" I could not hear the church bells.[5]

Thomas Hardy II died on 20 July 1892 (*Tess of the d'Urbervilles* having been published the previous November,) from which time the family business was carried on by his younger son (Hardy's brother) Henry. That Christmastime, it was apparent that Hardy was experiencing problems with his mail. Referring the the postmen's 'Christmas fuddlings,' he declared, 'Letters have already begun to behave very queerly. My proofs wander away to Scotland out of pure festivity, it seems, before they come to me from London.'[6]

Hardy's prodigious literary output continued unabated with *Jude the Obscure* (published on 1 November 1895.) A letter to publishers Harper & Brothers that December reveals him to be once again under attack from the critics:

I write... respecting *Jude* [i.e. *Jude the Obscure*]. I am much surprised, & I may say distressed, by the nature of the attack on it in the N.Y. [New York] *World,* which has just come into my hands.' [However, as far as Britain was concerned,] 'You will probably know that it [*Jude*] has been received here with about equal voices for & against – somewhat as Tess [*Tess of the d'Urbervilles*] was received.[7]

Said Hardy on December 30, 1896,

I have been all right in health, and have had a Christmas of the dull kind, which contents so-called "pessimists" like me – in its freedom from positive sorrow. An old choir of waits [street singers of Christmas carols] however, came from a village a few nights ago, & sang to us the same carols that used to be sung by the 'Mellstock' choir – (the characters that I like best in my own novels.)[8]

'…our Christmas & New Year here [at Max Gate] have been quite uneventful, except by post,' declared Hardy on New Year's Day, 1897.' It was his view, '…that a Christmas which brings no tragedies is upon the whole a thing to be thankful for when you have passed the time of life for expecting positive joys.'[9] That March (the year of Queen Victoria's diamond jubilee,) saw the publication of *The Well-beloved*.

Although Hardy had been writing poems for many years, it was not until December 1898 that his first book of verse, entitled *Wessex Poems*, was published. These reflect, time and again, disillusionment and lost love, an expression of his own sorrow and inner turmoil over the failure of his relationship with his wife Emma.

At Christmastime 1899, Hardy indicated to his friend, the novelist Florence Henniker (born 1855 - whom he first met in Dublin in January 1893) that his thoughts were very much with the Dorset Regiment, which had gone out to fight in the South African War: (where Florence's husband, Major Arthur Henniker-Major was serving as commander of the 2nd Battalion of the Coldstream Guards.)

This Imperial idea is, I fear, leading us into strange waters. I always imagined the business [of defeating the Boers] w'd [would] take us 3 years, rather than 3 months & I still adhere to my opinion.[10]

THE IMAGERY OF CHRISTMAS

Hardy's fascination with the Christmas Story and its imagery never left him. This is demonstrated in *Tess of the d'Urbervilles*, when William Dewy manages to escape from an aggressive bull, by pretending it is Christmas Eve!

Once there was an old aged man over at Mellstock – William Dewy by name - one of the family that used to do a good deal of business as tranters over there.... I knowed the man by sight, as well as I know my own brother, in a manner of speaking. Well, this man was acoming home–along from a wedding where he had been playing his fiddle, one fine moonlight night, and for shortness' sake he took a cut across Forty-acres, a field lying that way, where a bull was out to grass. The bull seed [saw] William, and took after him, horns aground, begad; and though William runned his best, and hadn't *much* drink in him, he found he'd never reach the fence and get over it in time to save himself. Well, as a last thought, he pulled out his fiddle as he runned, and struck up a jig, turning to the bull, and backing towards the corner. The bull softened down, and stood still, looking hard at William Dewy, who fiddled on and on; till a sort of smile stole over the bull's face.

This strategy seemed to work, but William found that as soon as he stopped playing and attempted to climb over the hedge, 'the bull would stop his smiling and lower his horns towards the seat of William's breeches.' Having been forced to play on until about 4 o'clock in the morning, William decided that there was only one way to save himself.

'There's only this last tune between me and eternal welfare! Heaven save me, or I'm a done man.' Well, then he called to mind

how he'd seen the cattle kneel o' Christmas Eves in the dead o'
night. It was not Christmas Eve then, but it came into his head to
play a trick upon the bull. So he broke into the 'Tivity [Nativity]
Hymn, just as at Christmas carol-singing; when, low and behold,
down went the bull on his bended knees, in his ignorance, just as
if 'twere the true 'Tivity night and hour. As soon as his horned
friend were down, William turned, clinked off like a long-dog, and
jumped safe over hedge, before the praying bull had got on his feet
again to take after him. William used to say that he'd seen a man
look a fool a good many times, but never such a fool as that bull
looked when he found his pious feelings had been played upon,
and 'twas not Christmas Eve....[1]

* * *

The nativity scene in the stable is recalled once more by Hardy in
his poem *The Oxen*:

Christmas Eve, and twelve of the clock.
'Now they are all on their knees,'
An elder said as we sat in a flock
By the embers in hearthside ease.

We pictured the meek mild creatures where
They dwelt in their strawy pen
Nor did it occur to one of us there
To doubt they were kneeling then.

So fair a fancy few would weave
In these years! Yet, I feel,
If someone said on Christmas Eve,
'Come; see the oxen kneel

'In the lonely barton by yonder coomb
Our childhood used to know,'
I should go with him in the gloom,
Hoping it might be so.

55

Although this poem is ostensibly about whether the oxen did literally kneel down on Christmas Eve, the last line, 'Hoping it might be so' raises the question as to whether it has a deeper meaning? Is this a hope on Hardy's part that the Biblical account of Jesus Christ's nativity is really true, even though he cannot quite bring himself to believe in the veracity of it?

'THE GRAVE BY THE HANDPOST:
A CHRISTIAN REMINISCENCE'

In his story *The Grave by the Hand Post* (published in 1897 – a handpost being a signpost on which the finger of a hand points the direction,) Hardy recorded an act of charity, when, one Christmas Eve, the band (quire) of the village of 'Chalk-Newton' (Hardy's name for Maiden Newton) encountered some men from the neighbouring village of 'Sidlinch' (Sydling St Nicholas) burying the body of the late Sergeant Samuel Holway, who had committed suicide. (It was an ancient custom that those who had committed suicide were to be buried not in a churchyard but at a crossroads, with a wooden stake driven through their heart.)

Quire member Lot Swanhills described his feelings in a conversation with Richard Toller, the hautboy (oboe) player:

'Tis hard upon a man, and he a wold [old] sojer [soldier], to serve en so, Richard. Not that the sergeant was ever in a battle bigger than would go into a half-acre paddock, that's true. Still, his soul ought to hae [have] as good a chance as another man's, all the same, hey?

Richard replied that he was quite of the same opinion. 'What d'ye say to lifting up a carrel [carol] over his grave, as 'tis Christmas, and no hurry to begin down in parish, and 'twouldn't take up ten minutes and not a soul up here to say us nay, or know anything about it?'

Having reached a consensus that this was the best course of action, the quire, thereupon placed themselves in a semicircle by the newly stirred earth, and roused the dull air with the well-known Number Sixteen of their collection, which Lot gave out as being the one he thought best suited to the occasion and the mood:-

'He comes' the pri'-soners to' re-lease',
In Sa'tan's bon'dage held'.

'Jown it – we've never played to a dead man afore,' said Ezra Cattstock, when, having concluded the last verse, they stood reflecting for a breath or two. 'But it do seem more merciful than to go away and leave en, as they t'other fellows have done.'

Finally, Ezra goes to Chalk-Newton rectory and makes arrangements for the body to be transferred to the Chalk-Newton churchyard.[1]

In this short story, Hardy shows his humanity, by recognizing the fact that although the sergeant had committed suicide (which in those days was an illegal act,) nevertheless, his soul should have as good a chance of going to Heaven as anybody else's.

A NEW CENTURY

The momentous occasion of the advent of a new century was recorded in *The Dorset County Chronicle*, when on Christmas Eve 1899, muffled peals and changes were rung at intervals on the bells, both of St Peter's Church and of Fordington St George, and the Volunteer Band - under Bandmaster J Stevens - played in the streets. Shortly before 11, the light shining in St Peter's Church reminded the passers-by of the watchnight service about to begin....

After the hour of midnight had struck, and the church bells had solemnly knelled the departure of the old year, they burst out into cheery peals to welcome in the new-peals in which every note of melancholy was swallowed up in full hearted joy.'[1]

As the years rolled by, Hardy became increasingly nostalgic for the past, as in the winter of 1901, when he wrote this heartrending poem entitled *Bereft*, in which he appears to be grieving at the loss of a male person – possibly his father, who had died 9 years earlier in 1892.

> In the black winter morning
> No light will be struck near my eyes
> While the clock in the stairway is warning
> For five, when he used to rise.
>
> Leave the door unbarred,
> The clock unwound,
> Make my lone bed hard –
> Would 'twere underground!

When the summer dawns clearly,
And the appletree-tops seem alight,
Who will undraw the curtain and cheerly
Call out that the morning is bright?

Hardy described the winter of 1903 as, 'dull enough... at this twilight time of the year.' The dead were continually in his thoughts. Christmas he said, was not, 'much to me nowadays, except as a raiser of "frustrate [disappointing] ghosts", of which the train grows longer every year, with no corresponding increase of flesh & blood companions to balance them.' Was this in part an expression of regret for the fact that he and Emma had no children?[2]

Hardy's mother Jemima, died on the Easter Sunday of 1904 aged 90. On 21 December of that year, Hardy wrote to novelist Sir Henry Rider Haggard, thanking him, 'heartily for the Christmas present of pheasants you have been so kind as to send...,' but regretting the fact that he was unable to send something, 'off my own property' by return. He explained that, 'a freehold estate of under 2 acres [i.e. Max Gate] does not yield any game larger than sparrows & starlings,' he said, 'except one hare which haunts our lawn, & will not be driven away, knowing that there is nobody here with a gun.'

A few days before Christmas 1905, Hardy, in his customary seasonal letter to Florence Henniker, declared that here (i.e. in Dorset), 'old fashioned sentiment lives on as long as anywhere – at any rate on such questions as killing a host of harmless animals to eat gluttonously of, & drinking quarts of liquor, by way of upholding the truths of Christianity.'[3]

The following Christmas, Hardy, wrote again to Florence Henniker, employing the use of imagery for which he was famous, 'I have received your pretty reminder of the season [presumably a Christmas card featuring birds.] We get plenty of such feathered choristers round our windows just now, since the weather has got colder.'[4] That New Year's Eve, Hardy wished Edmund Gosse a happy New Year. For himself however, the occasion would be far from happy. 'I am a prisoner in the house – having in fact got up to breakfast this morning for the first time for several days, owing to a chill I caught in some way just before Xmas Eve.'[5]

To Florence Henniker on New Year's Eve 1907, Hardy wrote, 'It is dreadfully dull here [i.e. at Max Gate] just now: raw, a little snow on the ground....' and he ends the letter, 'Your affecte [affectionate] & rather gloomy friend Tho. H.'[6] Hardy's letter to Florence Henniker of Christmas Eve 1909 contained similar sentiments:

After returning here [to Max Gate] from London a cold developed, & I have been laid up with a sore throat for a week or more. It has nearly gone off now, but I must stay indoors a few days longer; so my Christmas will be dull enough. Well a Merry Christmas to you & your house ("Merry" is the old word, & I like it best.) Ever affectionately Tho. H.[7]

In June 1910, Hardy's name appeared in the Birthday Honours List as a recipient of the Order of Merit. That November, he received the additional honour of being granted the freedom of his native county town of Dorchester. His Christmas however, was overshadowed by the death of 'Kitsey' the 'study cat', who was accustomed to sleeping, 'on any clean sheets of paper,' and 'to be much with me.'[8]

In 1912, Hardy's siblings Henry, Katharine and Mary (none of whom ever married,) left the family home at Higher Bockhampton ['Hardy's Cottage'] and moved into a large house Talbothays Lodge (designed by Hardy himself and built by his brother Henry,) situated a mile or so east of Max Gate. Hardy's Cottage now reverted to the Kingston Maurward Estate.

Hardy had no desire to drive a motor vehicle. Therefore in 1912, Harold Lionel Voss (grandson of Thomas Voss of Higher Bockhampton, who featured under his real name in *Under the*

Greenwood Tree,) an employee of Tilley's garage at Dorchester was, selected to drive Mr Hardy, and became his most regular hired chauffeur from then until 1914 [i.e. when war broke out,] and again from 1919 to the year before his [Hardy's] death in 1928.[9]

The Christmas of 1912 was overshadowed for Hardy by the death of his wife Emma on 27 November, 3 days after her 72nd birthday. Hardy told Florence Henniker that the event had taken him completely by surprise:

Emma's death was absolutely unexpected by me, the doctor, & everybody, though not sudden, strictly speaking. She was quite well a week before, & (as I fancy) in an unlucky moment determined to motor to some friends about 6 miles off. During the night following she had a bad attack of indigestion, which I attributed to the jolting of the car. She was never well from that time, though she came down to tea with some callers on the Monday evening before her death on Wednesday morning. I was with her when she passed away. Half an hour earlier she had told the servant that she felt better. Then her bell rang violently, & when we went up she was gasping. In five minutes all was over.

I have reproached myself for not having guessed there might be some internal mischief at work, instead of blindly supposing her robust & sound & likely to live to quite old age.[10]

Again, to Florence Henniker on 21 December 1913, Hardy revealed that Emma's death was still very much on his mind:

The new Christmas does not exhilarate me much. But of course I cannot expect it to. The worst of a sad event [the death of Emma] in middle life & beyond is that one does not recover from the shock as in earlier years; so I simply say to myself of this Christmas, 'Yet another!'[11]

On 10 February 1914, Hardy married Florence Emily Dugdale, a book reviewer and writer of children's books, whom he had first met 10 years previously.

HARDY: AN OPPONENT OF ALTERATION AND 'RESTORATION'

Despite his scepticism about Christianity, Hardy was a doughty protector of what he regarded as the country's ecclesiastical heritage. For example, in December 1889, he expressed his concern to Hugh Thackeray Turner, architect and Secretary to The Society for the Protection of Ancient Buildings, about a rumour he had heard, 'that the Church of the Village of Stratton, 2 or 3 miles from Dorchester, is about to be pulled down. I am not personally acquainted with the details of the building,' he said, 'but those who know its features inform me that judicious repair is all that is really necessary. It is a quaint little church, & it would be a thousand pities if it were destroyed.'[1]

Hardy had learnt from his forebears about the unhappy events which had afflicted Stinsford Church in the early 1840s. He had also experienced at first hand as an architect, a similar desecration at St Juliot [where he had first met Emma.]

In 1909, he told the Stinsford Church Restoration Committee that when it came to the subject of, what is called 'Church restoration', it should be borne in mind that the only legitimate principal for guidance is to limit all renewals to *repairs for preservation*, and never to indulge in alterations. It [Stinsford Church] is an interesting building, and one very easy to injure beyond remedy.

With regard to the creation of music at the church: If an Organ be really required I should say, speaking for myself alone, that the old west gallery should be re-erected for it. Its reconstruction would be inexpensive. [Then wistfully, as if remembering the old days of the Stinsford Choir:] Such west galleries, which were inadvisably destroyed in the last century are now getting replaced in some churches....[2]

In February 1910, Hardy was asked by Thackeray Turner for his comments on whether a proposal to lengthen the chancel of Puddletown Church was justified. As might be expected, Hardy was vigorous in his defence of the building:

Since the receipt of your letter I have enquired about the size of the congregation usually at the services, & I am told by two persons who frequently attend that the building is never full, & seldom half-full. The church is the only one I know in the county that has not been tampered with, & I agree with you in deploring the contemplated enlargement. I think this is a case in which the Society should exert itself [i.e. in opposing the proposed expansion.][3]

Sadly on this occasion, Hardy was unsuccessful in his endeavours, as indicated in a subsequent letter to Thackeray Turner that October, in which he regretted that, ...notwithstanding the endeavours of the Society & of others interested... I am only able to say that in passing Puddletown Church about 10 days ago I saw that the Chancel had been pulled down, also the east wall of the North Aisle; the adjoining arch, being endangered by these demolitions, was propped up. Gravestones had been removed from the churchyard, an extensive clearing made & foundations dug; & window tracery & other Gothic detail lay scattered about the churchyard.[4]

WARTIME CHRISTMASES

On Christmas Day 1914 (World War I having commenced on 4 August,) Hardy observed that, Dorchester is more or less full of soldiers & German prisoners, & I suppose this sort of thing will go on for a long time yet, for I see no prospects of any conclusion to the war.[1] A few days later, he said:

I do not recollect the end of any year which has been so full of uncertainty & gloom. To look forward to February… as the time when fighting will be renewed on a large scale, is not exhilarating. We have just helped to give a Christmas tree & presents to 550 soldiers' children.[2]

Hardy's sister Mary died on 24 November 1915 at Talbothays aged 73. In early December, Hardy declared,

I miss my sister very much. In childhood she was almost my only companion – the others being younger - & she had always been the one with the keenest literary tastes & instincts. She could paint a good likeness, too – particularly of women….[3]

Mrs A Stanley was cook to the Hardy household from 1916 to 1918. She recalled how Hardy could be somewhat parsimonious:

At Christmastime on Boxing Day, the postman, as was the custom then, called for his Christmas box, and I gave him 2/6 [two shillings and sixpence] for the family. When I saw Mr Hardy and told him and asked for the 2/6 he would not pay me. He said: 'Dorchester people never give tips.' I thought this funny as I had come from London where they did, but I quickly learned that

Dorset people, at least most of them, gave tips and are as generous as London people. Hardy was one of the rare exceptions.[4]

Just prior to Christmas 1916, Hardy told Florence Henniker: 'Our blackbirds & thrushes have had a hard time on account of the frost & snow, but they are recovering now,' he said. He also mentioned that a poem of his was shortly to be published entitled, *A New Year's Eve in War Time*. (This poem prophesied, 'More Tears! - More Famine & Flame - More Severance and Shock!')[5]

On New Year's Eve 1917, Hardy stated: 'Went to bed at 11. East wind. No bells heard.'[6] To Hardy the sound of the church bells ringing the new year in was always a great joy. However, on this occasion the bells were silent, presumably because of the fact of the war being in progress.

With the war still in progress, Hardy stated in early New Year 1918, 'We are doing what little we can down here, among other things getting up a play for Jan. 31 on behalf of the Dorsets in Mesopotamia.' This is a reference to the Dorset Regiment; the play referred to being *The Mellstock Quire* (an adaptation of Hardy's *Under the Greenwood Tree*.)[7] According to his wife Florence: 'The war destroyed all Hardy's belief in the gradual ennoblement of man, a belief he had held for many years....'[8] World War I ended on the eleventh day of the eleventh month, 1918.

ROLE REVERSAL: THE CHOIR NOW SERENADES HARDY

In 1893, Hardy had recorded that he and Emma spent Christmas at Max Gate as usual, and had received the carol-singers there on Christmas Eve where, 'though quite modern, with a harmonium, they made a charming picture with their lanterns under the trees, the rays diminishing away in the winter mist.' The wheel had now turned full circle, Hardy himself once having been one of their number.[1]

This tradition was continued even after the death of Hardy's first wife Emma, as WGL Parsons, who left school in 1919 and became a telegraph messenger boy in Dorchester, describes. Parsons, in the autumn of 1917, was given the opportunity by the Hardy Players, to take part in the Hardy play *Mellstock Quire*, which was to be presented in the Corn Exchange, Dorchester, in the early part of 1918.[2] The two performances duly took place on Thursday 31 January 1918,

the proceeds being in aid of "The Comforts Fund of the 1/4th Dorset Regiment" – but so successful was the production and so many people being unable to be accommodated for the performances that it was decided to give a third performance on the following evening, when again the Corn Exchange was filled to capacity.[3]

For the Thursday matinée performance, 'Mr and Mrs Hardy were among the appreciative audience....' After the performance Hardy observed that the boy choristers were, 'wearing the smocks which were worn by my father.' [i.e. Thomas II, and which he, Hardy, had presumably lent them.] 'Don't you agree that they have worn well?' he said.[4]

The following Christmas time, the choir of St Peter's Church, Dorchester, of which Parsons was a member, sang some of the more traditional carols at the door of Max Gate and we were all hospitably entertained by Mr and Mrs Hardy. During our partaking of welcoming warm drinks and biscuits Mr Hardy talked to us of his own interest in music and produced very proudly a 'cello which he explained his father had played in Gloucester Cathedral. Despite his quiet voice, he obviously was very delighted, as was Mrs Hardy and appreciative of our visit. [However,] The interior of Max Gate, as much of it as we had seen, did not impress my young mind very favourably I must confess. The heavy dismal and dark appearance, despite my seat being just below the lounge window, and our carols having been sung during the afternoon hours of daylight, coupled with the pale faces of both Mr and Mrs Hardy and their dark attire, was, to me, somewhat awesome; yet I can recall well how Mrs Hardy saw to Mr Hardy's requirements, be they for his musical instruments from another part of the room, or more refreshments. He was not required to 'fetch and carry' for himself, and she had the sweetest of manner and smile when plying us boys with more tea and cakes! As they shook us by the hand as we left it was a thrilling moment for we two 'Counterpoint Boys' of 'The Mellstock Quire' for words of recognition passed between us all. These Christmastide visits with the Church Choir continued until 1926....[5]

THE POST-WAR YEARS

In December 1919, Hardy opened the Bockhampton Reading Room and Club, which would be that village's memorial to the fallen of the War. For a performance in November 1920 of *The Return of the Native* by the Dorchester Dramatic society, Hardy provided the dramatist Alderman Mr Tilley, with 'the complete words of the old mumming play from which speeches are quoted in the novel.'[1] This he referred to in a letter, sent soon afterwards, to Sir Haymo Thornycroft, sculptor, in which he stated that,

The mumming interlude was especially attractive. I wonder if your St George's play in Cheshire was like ours here (the old Dorset version.) The presentation & wording differ in almost every county, though the general groundwork is much the same. Some versions are loaded with all sorts of absurdities....[2]

When Hardy wrote to Florence Henniker in December 1920, the mummers were again a topic of conversation:

Our Christmas threatens to be quite an old fashioned one. For some reason best known to themselves the Dorchester Mummers & carol singers are coming here on Christmas night, & we have to entertain them after their performance. I wish you could see the mumming: it is an exact reproduction of the Dorset mumming of 100 years ago, as described in 'The Return of the Native'.[3]

Sure enough, said Hardy's wife Florence, the carol singers and mummers came to Max Gate as they had promised, the latter performing the *Play of St George* just as he [Hardy] had seen it performed in his childhood.[4]

That New Year's Eve 1920, saw the publication of Hardy's appropriately named poem '*At the Entering of the New Year*', where once again there was singing and music making:

> Our songs went up and out the chimney,
> And roused the home-gone husbandmen;
> Our allemands, our heys, poussettings,
> Our hands-across and back again...
> Sent rhythmic throbbings through the casements
> On to the white highway...
>
> The contrabasso's measured booming
> Sped at each bar to the parish bounds,
> To shepherds at their midnight lambings,
> To stealthy poachers on their rounds;
>
> And everybody caught full duly
> The notes of our delight,
> As Time unrobed the Youth of Promise
> Hailed by our sanguine sight.

Miss Ellen E Titterington (known as Nellie) was the parlour maid from 1921 to 1928, and she gives an interesting insight into the life of the Hardy household:

Max Gate in winter was a grim, cold house. It only had open fireplaces with very small fires. Mr Hardy would not permit good fires. The best was in the kitchen, where he rarely came. When it was very cold his bedroom was heated with an oil stove, but when he was ill, with a coal fire.

He lived a rather stingy life. For instance, at Christmas Mr Hardy left on the table 2s. 6d. each for the cook and myself in small envelopes with our names written on the outside. Cook thought half-a-crown an insulting amount and indignantly refused to take it and left it on the table, and as she was my superior, I also left my envelope. Later in the day Mrs Hardy made the sums up to 10/- [ten shillings] each. He was very careful to avoid waste, and to see, as he thought, too much coal on the fire greatly disturbed him. The memory of his early days, when he was poor, must have remained with him and influenced his behaviour.[5]

Always a meticulous observer of the anniversaries of those who were near and dear to him, Hardy on 27 November 1922 recorded in his notebook, 'E's [Emma's] death-day, ten years ago. Went with F. [Florence] and tidied her [Emma's] tomb and carried flowers for her and the other two tombs.' (The latter was a reference to the tombs of the Hardy family, who, like Emma, were buried in Stinsford churchyard.)[6]

On 20 July 1923, the Prince of Wales (later King Edward VIII) visited the Hardy's for lunch at Max Gate. On December 30, said Florence,

Mr and Mrs G Bernard Shaw and Colonel TE Lawrence [of Arabia, who had enlisted earlier that year as a private soldier in the Tank Training School at nearby Bovington under the assumed name of 'TE Shaw',] lunched with the Hardys and spent several hours with them.

The following day, New Year's Eve, Hardy recorded in his notebook, 'Heard the bells in the evening.' However, he, 'did not sit up [i.e. to see the New Year in].'[7]

Despite the passing of the years, the memory of World War I remained fresh in Hardy's mind, as evidenced by a poem he wrote entitled *Christmas: 1924*, where he contrasts the Christmas message on the one hand, with the reality of war on the other:

> 'Peace upon Earth!' was said. We sing it,
> And pay a million priests to bring it.
> After two thousand years of mass
> We've got as far as poison-gas.

On 26 December 1924, Hardy declared: 'We have been as cheerful as may be this Christmas.... But I long ago entered the region in a lifetime in which anniversaries [presumably a reference to Christmas Day] are the saddest days of the year.'[8] That New Year's Eve, Hardy recorded in his notebook: 'Sat up and heard Big Ben and the London church bells by wireless ring in the New Year.'[9] Technology, it seemed, had arrived at Max Gate!

23 December 1925 was the birthday of Hardy's beloved late sister Mary. 'She came into the world… and went out… and the world is just the same… not a ripple on the surface left,' he wrote.[10] This was not strictly true, for apart from anything else, Mary had left behind some of her beautiful painted portraits of members of the family, without which our knowledge of them would have been that much the less.

To the Reverend Henry Cowley (Vicar of Stinsford since 1911,) Hardy, on 23 February 1926 presented his observations on a report by the bellfounders (those who cast the bells) on the bells of Stinsford Church:

1. As the Parish is not a rich one, could the difficulty & expense of recasting the treble [bell] be got over by cutting out the crack, as was done, I believe, with "Big Ben"? [the bell of the clock in St Stephen's Tower at the Palace of Westminster]. Even if the tone thus recovered should not be inferior to that of a new bell, there would the great advantage of retaining the actual old bell, which is of pre-Reformation date.

2. Could not some of the oak from the old beams & bell-carriages be re-used, as it can scarcely be entirely decayed.

3. It is understood that, in re-hanging, the canons [metal loops at the top of the bells by which they are hung] need not be cut off from the heads of the bells, which would be fastened to the head-stocks [the blocks of wood from which the bells are hung] in the old manner. As they would not be re-hung for ringing peals, there would be no object in mutilating them in the modern fashion to make them swing more easily.

If anything could be done, said Hardy, then 'I will subscribe something. I wish I could afford to pay for the whole job.'[11] Four days later, again to the Reverend Cowley, he wrote concerning the forthcoming appeal for the repair of the bells of Stinsford Church. 'They are in a wretched condition & the old oak bell-carriages & mechanism quite decayed. The tenor is of very fine tone, & the treble, which is cracked, is of pre-Reformation date.'

On 1 November 1926, Hardy paid his last visit to the cottage at Bockhampton where he was born. In the same month, Colonel TE Lawrence, his great friend, called in to say goodbye, as he had been posted to India with The Royal Air Force. Lawrence was described by Florence Emily Hardy as, 'one of his [Hardy's] most valued friends.'[12] Said Florence Hardy:

The year [1926] drew quietly to an end. On 23 December, a band of carol-singers from St Peter's, Dorchester, came to Max Gate and sang to Hardy, "While Shepherds Watched" to the tune which used to be played by his father and grandfather, a copy of which he had given to the rector. A sadness fell upon the household, for Hardy's dog Wessex, now thirteen years old was ill, and obviously near his end. [According to parlour maid Ellen Titterington, the dog had originally belonged to Florence, who introduced him to Max Gate shortly before her marriage to Hardy in 1914.][13]

On 27 December, Hardy recorded,

Our famous dog 'Wessex' died at ½ past 6 in the evening, thirteen years of age.' Wessex was buried in the grounds of Max Gate, and the following night, Hardy observed, 'Wessex sleeps outside the house for the first time for thirteen years.[14]

A headstone was made, designed by Hardy, which bore the words,

THE
FAMOUS DOG
WESSEX
August 1913 – 27 Dec. 1926.

73

Faithful. Unflinching.[15]

Two days later, Hardy described Wessex as, our devoted (and masterful) dog.... We miss him greatly, but he was in such misery with swelling and paralysis that it was a relief when a kind breath of chloroform administered in his sleep by 2 good-natured Doctors (not vets) made his sleep an endless one.[16]

That New Year's Eve, Hardy 'Did not sit up.'[17]

FAITH AND PHILOSOPHY

Given that throughout his life, Hardy was intrigued by Christian tradition and imagery, it is pertinent to enquire as to what extent if any, he himself embraced the tenets of that particular faith.

***

Hardy was born into a Christian, Protestant family that took its religion seriously, as shown by the fact that as a small boy, he was, taken by his father to witness the burning in effigy of the Pope and Cardinal [Nicholas] Wiseman in the old Roman amphitheatre at Dorchester during the no-popery riots. (The cardinal, who had returned from Rome and in 1850 been appointed the first Archbishop of Westminster, now proposed that England be restored to Catholicism.)[1]

When Hardy was prematurely transferred by his parents from the Higher Bockhampton village school to a Nonconformist (Protestants dissenting from the Anglican Church) day-school in Dorchester, this was not because his parents were Nonconformists; it was in order that he might escape the clutches of Julia Augusta Martin of Kingston Maurward House, who having no children of her own, had developed what may be described as a 'crush' on the boy.

Later, as a student of architecture in Dorchester, Hardy had engaged in heated arguments with a colleague over the question of infant baptism: he being convinced through his study of the subject that adult baptism was preferable, presumably because it gave people the opportunity to choose whether they wished to embrace Christianity or not, rather than having it thrust upon them.

The clash of polemics between the two pupils in the office, sometimes reached such a pitch of clamour, that the architect's wife (the architect being Mr John Hicks, who was also Hardy's tutor) would send down a message from the drawing room... imploring them not to make so much noise.[2]

This indicates not only how seriously Hardy took the question of baptism (he himself having been baptized on 5 July 1840 in Stinsford Church,) but it may also indicate a certain resentment on his part, that he himself had been given no choice in the matter. (These arguments would resurface in his novel *A Laodicean* published in 1881.)

As a young man, Hardy considered entering the Church but decided against it, and as the years went by he became more and more convinced of his inability to adopt the Christian faith. In fact his views seem more in tune with those of the poet Algernon Charles Swinburne, whose *Hymn of Man* contains the lines, 'Glory to Man in the highest! for Man is the master of things'.

Nevertheless, as an adult, Hardy continued to attend church services and take a lively interest in church architecture. For example, to the Reverend Handley Moule (originally from Fordington, Dorchester and now Bishop of Durham,) he said, 'Owing, I suppose, to my early training in Gothic architecture I retain a vivid interest in our Cathedrals....' He then referred to a poem of his entitled *The Abbey Mason*, 'published in Harpers magazine about a year ago on the origin of the "Perpendicular" style – that pre-eminently English development of mediaeval genius – it [i.e. the style] seems to have been invented at Gloucester.'[3]

***

By January 1897, Hardy had become more forthright in his views:

What seems to me the most striking idea dwelt upon is that of the arrest of light & reason by theology for 1,600 years. The older the one gets, the more deplorable seems the effect of that terrible, dogmatic ecclesiasticism - Christianity so-called (but really Paulinism *plus* idolatry) – on morals & true religion: a dogma with which the real teaching of Christ has hardly anything in common.[4]

On Christmas Eve 1899, Hardy wrote a poem entitled *A Christmas Ghost-Story*, which raised profound questions about the seeming contradiction between what he called Jesus Christ's 'Law Of Peace' and the reality of war, in this case the South African War.

> South of the Line, inland from far Durban,
> A mouldering soldier lies – your countryman.
> Awry and doubled up are his gray bones,
> And on the breeze his puzzled phantom moans
> Nightly to clear Canopus: 'I would know
> By whom and when the All-Earth-gladdening Law
> Of peace brought in by that Man Crucified,
> Was ruled to be inept, and set aside?
> And what of logic or of truth appears
> In tacking 'Anno Domini' to the years?
> Near twenty-hundred liveried thus have hied,
> But tarries yet the Cause for which He died.

[Canopus – the second brightest star in the solar system.]

To the editor of *The Daily Chronicle*, dated Christmas Day 1899, Hardy in reference to the poem, described the feelings of his 'phantom of a slain soldier' as being, 'plaintive, embittered, and sad at the prevalence of war during a nominal ERA (era) of peace.' Also that the 'phantom' is, 'neither British nor Boer, but a composite, typical phantom,' who, 'may consistently be made to regret on or about Christmas Eve… the battles of his life and war in general….'[5]

Throughout his life, Hardy wrestled with the intellectual problems posed by the Christian doctrine: 'How happy our ancestors were in

77

repeating in all sincerity these articles of faith!' he said, referring to phrases from the Prayer Book such as, 'We have erred and strayed from Thy ways like lost sheep' and, 'My soul doth magnify the Lord'. However, it was his view that, we repeat the words from an antiquarian interest in them, and in a historic sense, and solely in order to keep a church of some sort afoot... we are pretending [therefore] what is not true: that we are believers. This must not be; we must leave. And if we do, we reluctantly go to the door, and creep out as it creaks complainingly behind us.[6]

In January 1907, Hardy's poem *The New Year's Eve* was published in which the writer has the audacity to question God himself:

'I have finished another year,' said God.
'In grey, green, white, and brown;
I have strewn the leaf upon the sod,
Sealed up the worm within the clod,
And let the last sun down.'

'And what's the good of it?' I said,
'What reasons made you call
From the formless void this earthly tread
When nine-and-ninety can be read
Why nought should be at all?'

However, although God appears to be surprised at this questioning of his views, nevertheless:

He sank to raptness as of yore,
And opening New Year's Day
Wove it by rote as theretofore,
And went on working evermore
In his unweeting way.

[unweeting = unwitting]

In the same month, Hardy declared: 'It is Feuerbach [Ludwig Andreas Feuerbach (1804-72) German philosopher] who says that

78

God is the product of man....' However, he (Hardy) could not quite bring himself to believe that the Universe was not susceptible to some kind of rational explanation, declaring that: on the other hand I quite enter into Spencer's [Herbert Spencer (1820-1903) philosopher] feeling, that it is paralyzing to think what if, of all that is so incomprehensible to us (the Universe) there exists no comprehension anywhere.[7]

Hardy's work *The Dynasts* (a monumental drama of the Napoleonic wars in three parts, nineteen acts, and thirty scenes,) is also an attempt by him to explain the mystery of what he describes as, 'this unintelligible world.'[8]

However, Hardy denied that he had a 'philosophy' as such, and stated that his beliefs were, 'merely what I have often explained to be only a confused heap of impressions, like those of a bewildered child at a conjuring show.'[9] On New Year's Eve 1901, he came to the conclusion that, 'After reading various philosophic systems, and being struck with their contradictions and futilities, I have come to this: *Let every man make a philosophy for himself out of his own experience.* He will not be able to escape using terms and phraseology from earlier philosophers, but let him avoid adopting their theories if he values his own mental life.'[10]

***

It was not only in his prose, but also in his poetry that Hardy revealed the difficulty that he had in embracing the Christian faith. This he seemed to regard as failure on his part, and poems such as *The Impercipient* reflect his deep sense of regret:

> That with this bright believing band
> I have no claim to be,
> That faiths by which my comrades stand
> Seem fantasies to me,
> And mirage–mists their Shining Land,
> Is a strange destiny.

79

Why thus my soul should be consigned
To infelicity,
While always I must feel as blind
To sights my brethren see,
Why joys they've found I cannot find,
Abides a mystery.'

LOOKING BACK ON CHRISTMAS

For all Hardy's doubts, the Christmas story was something that he could not wholly expunge from his mind, and it is a theme which occurs repeatedly in his books and in his poems. However, as well as revealing an intense nostalgia on Hardy's part for Christmases past, some of his poems also reflect his intense inner despondency, perhaps the consequence of his unhappy marriage to Emma, which as time went by, would become a union in name only. That these feelings become particularly acute at Christmas time, is demonstrated in *The Reminder*:

> While I watch the Christmas blaze
> Paint the room with ruddy rays,
> Something makes my vision glide
> To the frosty scene outside.
>
> There, to reach a rotting berry,
> Toils a thrush, - constrained to very
> Dregs of food by sharp distress,
> Taking such with thankfulness.
>
> Why, O starving bird, when I
> One day's joy would justify,
> And put misery out of view,
> Do you make me notice you!

In *A Nightmare, and the Next Thing:* Hardy's feelings are even more poignant:

> On this decline of Christmas Day
> The empty street is fogged and blurred:

The house-fronts all seem backwise turned
As if the outer world was spurned:
Voices and songs within are heard,
Whence red rays gleam when fires are stirred,
Upon this nightmare Christmas Day.

Nevertheless, despite his despondency, Hardy derived a certain pleasurable satisfaction from remembering the Christmases of times gone by, as in *The House of Hospitalities* for example, when he looks back with pleasure on a time when Christmas was celebrated in a traditional way:

Here we broached the Christmas barrel,
Pushed up the charred log-ends;
Here we sang the Christmas carol,
And called in friends.

Time has tired me since we met here
When the folk now dead were young,
Since the viands were outset here
And quaint songs sung.

Now no Christmas brings in neighbours,
And the New Year comes unlit;
Where we sang the mole now labours,
And spiders knit.

Yet at midnight if here walking,
When the moon sheets wall and tree,
I see forms of old time talking
Who smile on me.

HARDY'S LAST CHRISTMAS

On 11 December 1927, Hardy became ill. His wife Florence takes up the story:

On the morning of that day he sat at the writing-table in his study, and felt totally unable to work. This, he said, was the first time that such a thing had happened to him. From then on his strength waned daily…. He was anxious that a poem he had written, *Christmas in the Elgin Room*, should be copied and sent to *The Times*.[1]

In this poem, he appears to regret the fact that Jesus Christ was ever born, and to imply that the human race was happier in pre-Christian days:

> 'We are those whom Christmas overthrew
> Some centuries after Pheidias knew
> How to shape us
> And bedrape us
> And to set us in Athena's temple for men's
> view…

> 'For all these bells, would I were still
> Radiant as on Athenai's Hill.'
> - 'And I, and I!'
> The others sigh,
> 'Before this Christ was known, and we had men's
> good will.'

[Pheidias - Athenian sculptor, born circa 490 BC. Athena – the patron goddess of ancient Athens.]

According to Florence, Hardy 'continued to come downstairs to sit for a few hours daily, until Christmas Day. After that he came downstairs no more.' That Christmas Day, Hardy wrote to his old friend Sir Edmund Gosse,

I am in bed on my back, living on butter-broth & beef tea, the servants being much concerned at my not being able to eat any Christmas pudding, though I am rather relieved.[2]

On Boxing Day, he said that he had been thinking of the Nativity and of the Massacre of the Innocents, and his wife [i.e. Florence herself] read to him the gospel accounts…. He remarked that there was not a grain of evidence that the gospel story was true in any detail.

As the year ended a window in the dressing-room adjoining his bedroom was opened that he might hear the bells, as that had always pleased him. But now he said he could not hear them and did not seem interested. The weather was bitterly cold, and snow had fallen heavily, being twelve inches deep in parts of the garden. In the road outside there were snow-drifts that in places would reach a man's waist.

Towards the end, Hardy asked his wife to read to him from the gospels, and from the Rubáiyát of Omar Khayyám:

> Oh, Though who Man of baser Earth didst make,
> And ev'n with Paradise devise the Snake:
> For all the Sin wherewith the Face of Man
> Is blacken'd – Man's forgiveness give –
> and take!

The local doctor Sir Henry Head, who was also Hardy's friend, was summoned. However, 'the weakness increased daily'.

Publisher and author Walter Newman Flower (1879-1964)'s family home was at Fontmell Magna, near Shaftesbury, some 25 miles north of Hardy's home at Max Gate. It was 'before the First

World War' (1914-1918), said Flower, that he first met Hardy, and the two men became firm friends.[3] By the time of his early teens, said Flower, he: 'had reached the first stage of book loving. I came upon *Under the Greenwood Tree*. Not that any greenwood tree mattered very much to me then. It was Hardy's name on the cover that made me take the book from the [book]case and settle down with it in the big armchair.

'I read until I lost myself in the story. It was life — the life I knew. The life that was happening every day around me. Surely in these pages was my village of Fontmell Magna. And these carol singers appeared to be those who besieged our house every Christmas Eve. The same crusted characters at whom I had so often peered out by slightly pulling aside the blind so that I should not be observed.'

This was a reference by Flower to Hardy's collection of short stories entitled *A Few Crusted Characters* (published in *Harper's New Monthly Magazine* in 1891).

'The same people — just the same people - stamping about in the snow with their fluttering lanterns, waiting between, 'Hark the Herald Angels Sing' and 'Good King Wenceslas'. The same people waiting whilst my father went through the green baize doors that led into the brewery to fetch beer for them - big foaming jugs of beer.'[4]

'For several years past', Flower continued: 'it had been a privilege of mine to send Hardy his Christmas dinner — a turkey or a Chinese goose reared in my modest orchard. Some little time before we had had a joke about these Christmas dinners. He thought that the Chinese geese I sent him (so much more free from oil than the ordinary geese) made him bilious. "I feel on Boxing Day as if I had been out 'on the tiles'", he said. So we stuck to turkeys from that year on.'

'A few days after Christmas Florence Hardy wrote to tell me that T. H. had enjoyed his turkey to the extent that he had eaten a second helping. And she said that he was coming back [recovering] so well that he wanted me to know he was inviting me now to go to his 90th birthday party, because he knew he was going to live to 90!'[5] Sadly, however, this proved not to be the case, and Hardy died shortly after 9 p.m. on 11 January 1928. He was aged 87.

ABOUT THE AUTHOR

ANDREW NORMAN was born in Newbury, Berkshire, UK in 1943. Having been educated at Thornhill High School, Gwelo, Southern Rhodesia (now Zimbabwe) and St Edmund Hall, Oxford, he qualified in medicine at the Radcliffe Infirmary. He married in 1967 and has two children.

From 1972-83 Andrew worked as a general practitioner in Poole, Dorset, before a spinal injury cut short his medical career. He is now an established writer whose published works include biographies of Thomas Hardy, Agatha Christie, Winston Churchill, Enid Blyton, Beatrix Potter, T. E. Lawrence, Adolf Hitler, and Robert Mugabe. Andrew remarried in 2005.

Andrew's interest in Thomas Hardy arose from the fact that his paternal forebears came from the parish of Fordington (Dorchester), which is adjacent to Hardy's own parish of Stinsford. In fact, his ancestor John Norman's three sons were baptized by the Reverend Henry Moule, whose own son Horatio (known as 'Horace') became arguably Thomas Hardy's greatest friend.

NOTES

NB. Letters quoted are from *The Collected Letters* of Thomas Hardy, vols. 1-7. (eds. Richard Little Purdy and Michael Millgate.)

CHAPTER 1

1. Hardy, Thomas, *Under the Greenwood Tree or The Mellstock Quire*, p.41.
2. Ibid, p.40.
3. Ibid, p.42.

CHAPTER 2

1. Hardy, Florence Emily, *The Life of Thomas Hardy 1840-1928*, p.8.
2. Thomas Hardy to the Reverend E. J. Bodington, mid-February 1923.
3. Hardy, Thomas, *Under the Greenwood Tree or The Mellstock Quire*, pp.43-5

CHAPTER 3

1. Hardy, Florence Emily, *The Life of Thomas Hardy 1840-1928*, p.12.
2. Hardy, Thomas, *Under the Greenwood Tree or The Mellstock Quire*, pp.56-60.

CHAPTER 4

Hardy, Thomas, *Life's Little Ironies*, pp.238-40.

CHAPTER 5

1. Hardy, Florence Emily, *The Life of Thomas Hardy 1840-1928*, p.13.
2. Ibid, p.92.
3. Brown, Joanna Cullen, *Hardy's People: Figures in a Wessex Landscape,* p.266.
4. Hardy, Florence Emily, op. cit., p.429.
5. Cox, J Stevens (editor), *Monographs on the Life of Thomas Hardy: Motoring with Thomas Hardy*, by Harold Lionel Voss.
6. Dorset 1841 census.

CHAPTER 6

1. Hardy, Florence Emily, *The Life of Thomas Hardy 1840-1928*, p.12.
2. Ibid, pp.8-9.
3. Ibid, p.10.
4. Ibid, p.18.
5. Hardy, Thomas, *A Few Crusted Characters: Absent-mindedness in a Choir* (in *Thomas Hardy: Selected Short Stories*,) pp.241-4.

CHAPTER 7

1. Hardy, Thomas, *Under the Greenwood Tree or The Mellstock Quire*, p.58.
2. Hardy, Thomas, *A Few Crusted Characters: Absent-mindedness in a Choir*, (in Thomas Hardy: Selected Short Stories,) pp.241,244.
3. *Interview Fragments with Katharine Hardy*, in Cox, J Stevens and G Stevens Cox (editors), 1980, *The Thomas Hardy Yearbook, Number 10*, p.46.

CHAPTER 8

1. Hardy, Florence Emily, *The Life of Thomas Hardy 1840-1928*, p.8.
2. Ibid, pp.21-2.

3. Ibid, p.15.
4. Ibid, p.32.
5. Ibid, p.32.
6. Hardy, Thomas, *Under the Greenwood Tree or The Mellstock Quire*, pp.78,83.
7. Ibid, p.78.

CHAPTER 9

Hardy, Thomas, *Under the Greenwood Tree or The Mellstock Quire*, Preface.

CHAPTER 10

1. Archer, William, *Real Conversations*.
2. Thomas Hardy to Arthur Hopkins, 20 February 1878
3. Hardy, Thomas, *The Return of the Native*, p.158.
4.Ibid, p.128.
5. Hardy, Thomas, *The Dynasts*, Preface.
6. Ibid, Act 7, Scene 8.

CHAPTER 11

1. Thomas Hardy to Mary Hardy, 3 November 1862.
2. Hardy, Florence Emily, *The Life of Thomas Hardy 1840-1928*, p.212.
3. Florence Dugdale to Edward Clodd, 3 July 1913, Brotherton Library, Leeds.
4. Hardy, Evelyn. *Thomas Hardy: A Critical Biography*, p.143.

CHAPTER 12

1. Millgate, Michael (editor), *Letters of Emma and Florence Hardy*, pp.7-8.
2. Hardy, Florence Emily, *The Life of Thomas Hardy 1840-1928*, pp.124-5.

CHAPTER 13

1. Hardy, Florence Emily, *The Life of Thomas Hardy 1840-1928*, pp. 169-70.
2. *A Guide to St Peter's Church, Dorchester.* p.13.

CHAPTER 14

1. Hardy, Florence Emily, *The Life of Thomas Hardy 1840-1928*, p.176.
2. Cox, J Stevens (editor), *Monographs on the Life of Thomas Hardy: Thomas Hardy at the Barber's*, by W. G. Mills.
3. Hardy, Florence Emily, op. cit., p.184.
4. Thomas Hardy to Edmund Gosse, 24 December 1886.
5. Hardy, Florence Emily, op. cit., pp. 230-1.
6. Thomas Hardy to Lena Milman, 23 December 1892.
7. Thomas Hardy to Harper and Brothers, 24 December 1895.
8. Thomas Hardy to Florence Henniker, 30 December 1896.
9. Thomas Hardy to Agnes Grove, 1 January 1897.
10. Thomas Hardy to Florence Henniker, 19 December 1899.

CHAPTER 15

Hardy, Thomas, *Tess of the D'Urbervilles*, pp.90-91.

CHAPTER 16

1. Hardy, Thomas, *The Supernatural Tales of Thomas Hardy*, pp. 266-8.

CHAPTER 17

1. Chandler, James K, *Turning the Century with Thomas Hardy*, p.131-2.
2. Thomas Hardy to Edward Clodd, 22 December 1903.
3. Thomas Hardy to Florence Henniker, 21 December 1905.
4. Thomas Hardy to Florence Henniker, 21 December 1906.
5. Thomas Hardy to Edmund Gosse, 30 December 1906.

6. Thomas Hardy to Florence Henniker. 31 December 1907.

7. Thomas Hardy to Florence Henniker, Christmas Eve, 1909.

8. Thomas Hardy to Florence Henniker, 19 December 1910.

9. Cox, J Stevens (editor), *Monographs on the Life of Thomas Hardy: Motoring with Thomas Hardy*, by Harold Lionel Voss.

10. Thomas Hardy to Florence Henniker, 17 December 1912.

11.Thomas Hardy to Florence Henniker, 21 December 1913.

CHAPTER 18

1.Thomas Hardy to Thackeray Turner, 16 December 1889.

2. Thomas Hardy to the Stinsford Church Restoration Committee 25 April 1909.

3. Thomas Hardy to Thackeray Turner, 7 February 1910.

4. Thomas Hardy to Thackeray Turner, 8 October 1910.

CHAPTER 19

1. Thomas Hardy to the Reverend E. C. Leslie, 25 December 1914.

2. Thomas Hardy to S. Cockerell, 30 December 1914.

3. Thomas Hardy to Mary Sheridan, 7 December 1915.

4. Cox, J Stevens (editor), *Monographs on the Life of Thomas Hardy: Hardyana*, by Mrs A. Stanley.

5. Thomas Hardy to Florence Henniker, 22 December 1916.

6. Hardy, Florence Emily, *The Life of Thomas Hardy 1840-1928*, p.379.

7. Thomas Hardy to Dorothy Allhusen, 4 January 1918.

8. Hardy, Florence Emily, op. cit., p.368.

CHAPTER 20

1. Hardy, Florence Emily, *The Life of Thomas Hardy 1840-1928*, p.261.

2. Parsons, W. G. L., *A 'Mellstock Quire' Boy's Recollections of Thomas Hardy*, p.3.

3. Ibid, p.5.

4. Ibid, p.5.

5. Ibid, p.8.

CHAPTER 21

1. Thomas Hardy to Harold Child, 11 November 1920.
2. Thomas Hardy to Sir Haymo Thornycroft, 28 November 1920.
3. Thomas Hardy to Florence Henniker, 22 December 1920.
4. Hardy, Florence Emily, *The Life of Thomas Hardy 1840-1928*, p.411.
5. Cox, J. Stevens (editor), *Monographs on the Life of Thomas Hardy: The Domestic Life of Thomas Hardy 1921-1928*, by Miss E. E. Titterington.
6. Hardy, Florence Emily, op. cit., p.418.
7. Ibid, pp.423-4.
8. Thomas Hardy to A. C. Benson, 26 December 1924.
9. Hardy Florence Emily, op. cit., p.427.
10. Ibid, p.430.
11. Thomas Hardy to the Reverend H. G. B. Cowley, 23 February 1926.
12. Hardy, Florence Emily, op. cit., p.434.
13.Ibid, p.434.
14. Ibid, p.434.
14.Ibid, p.435.
15.Thomas Hardy to Harley and Helen Granville Barker, 29 December 1926.
16.Hardy, Florence Emily, op. cit., p.434.

CHAPTER 22

1. Hardy, Florence Emily, *The Life of Thomas Hardy 1840-1928*, p.21.
2. Ibid, p.29.
3. Thomas Hardy to the Reverend Handley Moule, 3 December 1913.
4. Thomas Hardy to Edward Clodd, 17 January 1897.
5. Thomas Hardy to editor of *The Daily Chronicle*, 25 Dec. 1899 (in Haining, *The Supernatural Tales of Thomas Hardy*, pp.286-8.)
6. Hardy, Florence Emily, op. cit., pp.332-3.
7. Thomas Hardy to Edward Clodd, 2 January 1907.

8. Hardy, Thomas, *The Dynasts*, Preface.
9. Hardy, Florence Emily, op. cit., p.410.
10. Ibid, p.310.

CHAPTER 24

1. Hardy, Florence Emily, *The Life of Thomas Hardy 1840-1928*, p.444.
2. Thomas Hardy to Sir Edmund Gosse, 25 December 1927.
3. Flower, Newman, *Just as it Happened*, p.86.
4. Ibid, p.83.
5. Ibid, p.103.

ACKNOWLEDGMENTS

I am grateful to Dorchester County Record Office; Dorset County Museum; The National Trust; Andrew Leah; Mark Davison; Professor Michael Millgate; Joan Jordan; Michael Dragffy.

The illustrations by R Knights are from the 1878 Edition of *Under The Greenwood Tree*, published by Chatto & Windus, London. This includes the choir and church spire (title page) and the Christmas bells (introductory page).

As always, I am deeply indebted to my wife Rachel, for all her help and encouragement.